An important and timely book by the
President of the University of Illinois
stressing the urgency of what must be
done to preserve and expand the qualities
and services of our educational system.

7/7/7'

WHAT PRIORITY FOR EDUCATION?

WHAT PRIORITY
FOR EDUCATION?

THE AMERICAN PEOPLE
MUST SOON DECIDE

by David D. Henry

UNIVERSITY OF ILLINOIS PRESS · URBANA · 1961

Believing that the discussions of higher education by the President of the University of Illinois will contribute to public understanding of current educational issues, the University of Illinois Foundation has joined in sponsoring the publication of this volume.

PREFACE

Although today there is probably more public discussion of education than ever before in the United States, the central issue — the primacy of education in the welfare of the nation — does not have adequate focus or sufficient emphasis.

Every university administrator must give extensive public interpretation to the needs of his institution. He knows, however, that the fulfillment of those needs will be dependent upon the climate of public attitudes toward education. That mood today is apathetic. It is imperative, therefore, that the public realize that decisions are being made by indecision, that the future is being determined by those not voting and by those not giving, and that unless the educational price is paid for progress there will be no progress. There isn't much time left to do those things necessary to keep open the college door and maintain quality and scope in the service of the colleges and universities of the nation.

During the past five years, I have spoken and written on this main theme many times, developing its parts as a backdrop for interpreting the needs of the University of Illinois. I have been encouraged to bring together the main points of these discussions in the hope that they may contribute to defining the issues in the current debate on education and perhaps to heightening the feeling of urgency as to what must be done and done quickly.

Much of the material in this book has appeared in print, but it has been edited to eliminate repetition and to achieve a degree of coherence. Additional sections have been added to give the book a larger unity of its own. For permission to reprint portions of addresses and articles I am indebted to those listed on page 88.

Although the public schools at the elementary secondary level are discussed, and indeed they cannot and should not be separated from the national appraisal of what to do about higher education, the chief emphasis in this book is upon higher education.

The first editing of the material here presented was the work of Mr. Raymond F. Howes, Staff Associate and Administrative Assistant, American Council on Education, assisted by Mrs. Eunice Parker, Research Associate, President's Office, University of Illinois.

I am indebted to Mr. Howes not only for the editing, but for his encouragement of the idea that what was prepared for the platform and oral presentation might also merit book presentation.

DAVID D. HENRY
The University of Illinois
Urbana, Illinois

CONTENTS

THE ISSUE

"What confronts us all is an enormous and unprecedented opportunity to develop the human resources of this Nation to a broader and fuller degree than even our most optimistic forebears ever dreamed of. The challenge presented by this opportunity points up, rather than supplants, the cardinal role of education. That role is to develop human beings of high character, of courageous heart and independent mind, who can transmit and enrich our society's intellectual, cultural and spiritual heritage, who can advance mankind's eternal quest for truth and beauty and who can leave the world a better place than they found it. Only by pursuing these paramount goals of education can we insure a free society and a sane and peaceful world in which all individuals may live in greater dignity and achieve greater fulfillment."[1]

NEEDED: A NEW SET OF
NATIONAL PRIORITIES

There is no more dramatic story than the working of the educational process in the lives of people. Education is the chief instrument of social and vocational mobility in American life, the formula for freedom which is our banner around the world. Education gives meaning to our faith in the central place of individual welfare, a concern which distinguishes our national mode from that of our antagonists in the world scene.

Consider the journey of the poor boy from the city slums to his position as business tycoon; the road traveled by the lad from the farm to the life of scholarship; the achievement of the minister's son as he makes a career as world diplomat; the development of the street urchin into the influential preacher; the change of the immigrant boy into the national leader.

If the meaning of education, as reflected in the transformation in the lives of people, were effectively communicated to the American people, the present state of suspense as to the future of education in this country would change into a state of action.

Three featured articles in a recent issue of *U. S. News and World Report*[1] provided a contrast which reflects our national uncertainty as to priorities and purposes:

One dealt with an economist's forecast for "an uproarious decade ahead." He said the period is sure to be one of growth, that the rate of economic development will be far more pronounced in the second half than in the first. He outlined 19 major premises to support his point.[2]

A second was entitled, "What People Are Spending Their Money for Now." The tabulation indicated there is record spending for travel, hobbies, luxuries and "good living," and that "after the necessities are paid for, people have more money than ever before for other things."[3]

Then, by contrast, an article in the same edition referred to a revolt by local taxpayers and to the problems of city and state governments to get sufficient money to carry on public services.[4]

Lip service is universally given to the importance of education in the expanding economy and to the national security. But there is confusion as to where the required expanding support is coming from and when.

There are those who say that education is so important that funds should be supplied without regard to present patterns of support or present relationships to the economy. This is the point of view of President Eisenhower's Science Advisory Committee. Its recent report notes that the United States spends about $18 billion a year on formal education (about 4% of the gross national product), and goes on to say: "If we wisely spent twice that much to achieve higher quality it would be more than worth the cost. Doubling our current annual investment in education is probably a minimal rather than an extravagant goal."

Others endorse the point with the oft-repeated comparison with expenditures on liquor, cosmetics and tobacco, concluding that anyone who questions the possibility of spending more on education simply has a distorted sense of national and community values.

Then there are those who support these premises, but who gravely shake their heads when it comes to voting for an increase in the philanthropic budget or encouraging an increase in state taxes.

And, finally, we have the Beardsley Rumls who believe that our only recourse is a complete change in both educational practice and financial policy. Mr. Ruml further advocates taking the control of education method and organization out of the hands of the professionals and turning it over to laymen.

A former member of the Parole Board of Illinois recently stated that it costs $1,000 per year to house and feed one male prisoner, $3,000 for one female prisoner.

Thus the cost to the State for a male prisoner exceeds the minimum cost for an undergraduate at the University of Illinois, and the cost for a female prisoner exceeds the cost for a graduate student.

Education expenditures are investments in the future. No improvement in our society is expected from the penal institutions. They are necessary, but they do not build the future.

Yet, while it is difficult to get the support needed for either education or corrections, one is about as readily supported as another in many states. Education does not have the kind of priority one would assume it would get.

The priorities must be changed. Unless the supply line of personnel and ideas from our colleges and universities keeps pace with the development in the economic life of our states and of the nation, the ultimate growth in the economy will be less than otherwise would be possible. Education is the source of supply of trained people, of specialists for management and operation, and of research for the advancement of basic knowledge and the application of that knowledge through new processes and new procedures.

It is a great problem in a growing and prosperous nation to have the public understand the relationship between education and prosperity, even security. We cannot have the last two without the first.

The point was never more eloquently phrased than by Walter Lippmann in his address to the National Citizens Committee for the Public Schools in March 1954. He said: "Our education effort . . . has not yet been raised to the plateau of the age we live in. . . . We must measure our educational effort as we do our military effort. That is to say, we must measure not by what it would be easy and convenient to do, but what it is necessary to do in order that the nation may survive and flourish. We have learned that we are quite rich enough to defend ourselves, whatever the cost. We must now learn that we are quite rich enough to educate ourselves as we need to be educated."[5]

Robert D. Calkins of the Brookings Institution has formulated the question of purposes and priorities in this way: "What we need for education and for this nation is a new sense of purpose in light of the realities, a new mission and a will to achieve it. Instead of being dragged to our future, we need above all else a vision of the possible and enthusiasm for the possible. This spirit should not have to be handed down from the White House, but should arise out of the hopes and determination of free men with a purpose. In such an atmosphere education can have a vital role and a glorious future."[6]

Chapter I

THE CRISIS IN THE PUBLIC SCHOOLS

Any discussion of any educational issue today must start with a consideration of the school system of the nation. For over a decade the percentage of the national income spent on schools has steadily declined, while in the same period the population of the country has increased and an unprecedented demand for extension of educational services has developed. Although the present physical conditions of the schools have been in the making for a long time, the inevitable results are only now becoming generally understood. Teacher salaries are inadequate to hold many of the present staff from competitive positions, inadequate to keep many others on the job with full time and with full energy, and inadequate as an inducement for recruitment. In thousands of instances, unsatisfactory working conditions so limit effectiveness that teachers know they are "keeping school," not "teaching school." Teacher and room shortages place hundreds of thousands of children in shortened shifts and countless numbers in oversized classes. A high percentage of high school and elementary pupils go to buildings rated unsafe from fire or only

"possibly" safe. Appalling makeshifts are numerous — in garages, basements, apartments and improvised halls.

These physical manifestations of poor school conditions are
dramatic and can be measured. There are equally serious short-
comings that cannot be measured. Only half of the students
who start school finish high school. There are as many of college
ability who do not go on to college as are enrolled. Many needs
for counselling service, vocational, mental hygiene, physical, academic, are unfilled.

The seriousness of the current school shortages is heightened
by the enrollment prospect in the years immediately ahead.
Elementary schools for several years have been filled beyond
capacity, and the bulge has progressed through the high schools,
and is now on the campuses of the colleges. All institutions face
the current load with inadequate staffs, insufficiently paid, with
a deficit in facilities, as well as in operating budgets. In the next
fifteen years, says President John Perkins of the University of
Delaware, "As much floor space will have to be provided for
higher education as was built in the three hundred previous
years of collegiate history." And the building need is but an
index to teacher need and to the need for operating resources.

"The general picture is that of a nation which has outgrown
the capacity of its school system," says Walter Lippmann. "Our
present expenditure is geared to an earlier age before the changes
in population, economics, and the requirements of the world
position of the United States."

The present crisis in the support of the schools is the third
within the last twenty-five years. The economic whirl of 1929
to 1933 was the first, and the lag in education recovery was
greater than in the other areas of public life, and the schools are
still suffering some of the consequences of having made only a
partial recovery at that time.

The second crisis in this span of two and a half decades came during World War II. Initially, the schools were considered unrelated to the war effort, and school activity was not classified as essential. It was only after a strenuous interpretative battle that schools took their proper place on the home front. Although the schools were later recognized as controlling in the effectiveness of civilian defense, civilian morale and specialized war training, some of the deficiencies in the present situation may be traced to that period of lack of understanding of the place of the schools in total war.

The current crisis is the third in this short time span and it comes at a time of prosperity. Ironically, the schools are suffering a dollar crisis in the most prosperous era in American history.

Why is it necessary for the schools to go through these short cycles of crisis and antidote? With the great American tradition for popular education, why does the lag in understanding create these dangerous deficits in dollars, teachers and facilities?

The majority of the American people have been to school for some period in their lives. Was their experience so unhappy or meaningless that they forever remain apathetic or antipathetic? We cannot believe so. Some cynics maintain that the failure in public support is an index to an alleged anti-intellectualism of today. Others say it is traceable to a short-sighted commercialism, or to a lack of cultural values.

The cynics, however, have not understood American history. The American people have always had great faith in the value of education, and they have it today. They believe in the social benefits of individual achievement that flow from the educated person. They have great faith in the worth of the American experience, and they are eager to have each generation come into an understanding of those elements in our culture which have been identified with national progress. They believe in the discovery of new ideas. They believe in the right of the individual to have an opportunity to develop according to his talents. They believe that effective democracy is dependent upon enlightened minds.

Why, then, the gap between creed and practice, between faith and fulfillment?

I

The complications of governmental structures often make it difficult for issues involving schools to become clear in a way that people may react to them separately from other public matters. The local community is subject to control by a variety of governmental units — city, town, township, county, school district, state and sometimes regional authority.

The cultural needs of the people are many times caught in this network. There are many examples where schools have been hampered by artificial boundaries, tax limitations and competitive jurisdictions; other public agencies devoted to cultural enterprise have been similarly inhibited by their organizational lines. In libraries and museums, in recreation, the problems are also particularly noticeable. There is also the point made by Mr. Vernon L. Heath that there is not too much local control of education but there is too much local control by too few people.

In the traditional evolutionary method of changing governmental practice in the United States, these problems of local government will ultimately be solved. Flexibility to meet changing times has been the genius of the American way at all levels of government. The time lag, however, will create a serious deficit in the educational and cultural potential unless the problem is meanwhile met by citizen enterprise.

If the educational and cultural pattern of a community is to be dynamic, responsive to the needs of the people, vital and creative, a civic *leadership* force must be utilized. This leadership must at all times be responsive to those who have legal and formal responsibilities but it supplements local government in the clarification of civic issues. The Allegheny conference in the Pittsburgh area is an example of such a group at work. Lesser known advisory citizen groups have rendered notable service. Such groups are not of the "pressure" variety, but rather problem-solving.

The so-called "pressure group" has its place in the democratic way, and is a constructive channel of group expression as long as the different pressure groups are in balance. "Democracy is a state of flux between pressure groups," said Will Durant.

The complexity of modern life, however, demands the steadiness of reasonableness within civic objective. A public opinion, off balance, rebounding from the shouting of partisans and the propaganda of selected facts does not make for civic responsibility.

Arrogance of opinion belongs to those who have no responsibility. It is the characteristic of the pressure group. The problem-solving group, on the other hand, must be dispassionate in its approach to community issues. It is to be regretted that there is a persistently angry tone in the discussion of American public affairs. Schools and school people must not submit to the fashion. In discussion and reconciliation of divergent points of view, schools and universities must, in attitude and tone and method, reflect the temper and quality of the scholarly way.

A school and civic leadership should be developed in each community, not for panaceas but for problem-solving, not just for "rescue operations" but for continuing support.

Basic to such development is a school leadership which believes in the wisdom of the people and in the community-centered school, and a civic leadership which is dedicated to school improvement.

Many school administrators fear such interaction with community leadership. Some do not know the techniques of group consultation; sometimes they think they will appear not to know their business; sometimes they fear citizen "interference" with professional management and thus the creation of more problems.

It has been amply demonstrated, however, that when the civic and school leadership understand their mission and work together for community understanding, the public then has a chance to exercise its responsibility for the public schools intelligently and effectively. Without clarity of issues and problems, the public, even with great faith in the schools, with great eagerness to support the schools, both financially and against attack, cannot find channels of expression.

Some time ago, I set down for my own guidance some precepts which occurred to me as appropriate guidelines for school administrators and for civic leaders interested in building effective schools.

TEN PRECEPTS FOR SCHOOL LEADERSHIP

To assist a community properly to exercise responsibility for its public schools, the school leadership:

1. Believes in community consultation and establishes formal and informal mechanisms for this task.

2. Believes that communication is two-way and treats seriously, discriminatingly, and nondefensively the criticisms and suggestions made.

3. Encourages continuous communication and goes to the people at all times on all subjects, not just at moments of crisis.

4. Believes broad public support is the outcome of friendly

staff attitudes and effective service and rejects press-agentry and politics as substitutes in community relations.

5. Stimulates community service beyond the stereotypes of traditional school offerings and in use of its facilities, in the encouragement of new programs, and in supporting non-school educational activities raises the level of community measures of educational values.

6. Lives by the concept that the schools are a social agency, and achieves its potential in the public service by an everlasting devotion to human values in every administrative and policy decision.

7. Not only remains neutral in the normal interest clashes of a community, but seeks to make the schools a common rallying point of all groups and thus be a force for community harmonization.

8. Initiates and encourages cooperation among the educational and cultural agencies of the community, public and private, and minimizes professional competition and conflict.

9. Does not hesitate to imitate the applicable good practices of other communities, but is ever alert to take advantage of local resources, both physical and intangible.

10. Accepts the public character of the schools, does all of its business in the public view, plays no favorites, and admits no cause for vulnerability on the grounds of special privilege or partisan interest, thus establishing community-wide acceptance of the schools' integrity and good faith.

TEN PRECEPTS FOR CIVIC LEADERSHIP

To assist a community properly to exercise its responsibility, the civic leadership:

1. Accepts the central place of youth in the dynamics of community life and encourages all agencies devoted to youth service.

2. Believes in the economic outcomes of an educated citizenry and is willing to invest funds accordingly.

3. Believes in the independence of school government and insists that it be both free and responsible in its mission.

4. Works for the political immunity of its schools.

5. Stands for fair play in the interpretation of controversial issues involving the schools and their staffs.

6. Responds unreservedly to calls for voluntary service and makes sure that lay participation in school affairs is representative and broadly based.

7. Respects school service as a profession and supports all school policies which underlie this concept.

8. Accepts the public nature of the schools and opposes individual or group advantage in business or professional affairs.

9. Believes in the importance of community appraisal, through established channels, and insists upon continuing review of all programs and policies.

10. Accepts the responsibility of keeping informed on school affairs and educational practices so that appraisal of school effectiveness may be logical and well-grounded.

With complete confidence in the process of democratic appraisal, school and civic leadership together can build a responsiveness in community life which is the shield of the school program, as well as a source of inspiration and benefaction. Again to quote Mr. Heath in his report on the Illinois Little White House Conferences: "There is no problem in public education that greater public understanding will not solve."

II

A second suggestion for eliminating the cycles in public understanding and support of the schools, has its root in an old idea much discussed twenty-five years ago under the theme, "Teaching the school as a social institution." Considerable effort has been given to making the school a curricular consideration, and in some places effective work has been done. Teaching the place of the schools in American life is more than a matter of giving information, however. Attitudes must be created by the fervor and dedication of a great profession.

We should begin now to prevent the next crisis in education, by examining carefully, at all levels, from elementary through college, where we teach the relationship of education to economic well-being, to public health, to the great values in the American way.

We must work to have every graduate understand, in a way appropriate to his level:

That the public school system, including the colleges and universities, provides cohesiveness in American life. Schools are the neutral ground where partisans on all other issues — religious, economic, political, social — may join in a common effort for improvement in the public welfare. The public schools belong to all the people, all the time, and must therefore have political immunity and complete social understanding and support.

That education is the mainspring of the dynamics of American growth. The education of the consumer, the training of the expert, the discovery in the research laboratory, the service of the professions, the preparation of the leader in all walks of life are indispensable to prosperity and economic and physical well-being.

That education is the foundation of effective national defense. Limited in manpower, America is dependent upon brain-power and technical effectiveness. From the discovery of new weapons to their use in the field, from the understanding and purpose of the smallest military unit to the strategy of the Joint Chiefs of Staff, national defense is an educational process and is built upon the effectiveness of the schools. Dependent upon a citizens' military force, individual understanding of the purpose of national defense is the heart of its success. Citizenship education is the first schooling of the good soldier in a democracy.

That education is the essence of the democratic hope. In providing "social mobility," education keeps alive the aspiration of every person that he and his children will have an opportunity to improve their lot. Democracy does not promise there will be no economic or cultural dividing lines. It *does* promise that everyone has a chance to cross such lines if he has the will and ability to do so. The schools are the symbol of that tradition for they are the means for continuing individual improvement.

That education is the sustenance of freedom. The inquiring mind, the searching spirit, the quest for new frontiers are the basic forces for freedom. Bounded only by integrity and honesty, the search for truth is ever to be encouraged.

That education is the means of the individual's spiritual and cultural fulfillment. "Man cannot live by bread alone" but only by development of his talents and understandings can he develop his own "good life" in relation to his fellow men and his God.

That education is the training ground for democratic action. The motivation of good citizenship begins in the schools and the identification of the responsibilities of leadership. The great traditions of the Republic must be the inspiration for continuing citizenship responsibility.

In addition to these postulates, we must also teach how education is organized. If the citizen is to understand how to participate in supporting his schools, he must know the reasons for separate school government, local control, state participation, who runs our schools and why. In these points we have both a curriculum and a creed, a platform and a goal. It will win support where the "let's feel sorry for the teacher" approach is bound to fail.

The time is at hand for a resurgence of America's faith in

public education: the faith expressed by Jefferson when he said, "If a nation expects to be ignorant and free, it expects what never was and never will be"; the faith expressed by the Ordinance of 1787, "Religion, morality, and knowledge being necessary to good government and the happiness of mankind, schools and the means of education shall forever be encouraged"; the faith expressed by James Russell Lowell, America's accepted poet laureate, one hundred years ago, "It was in making education not only common to all, but in some sense compulsory on all, that the destiny of the free republics of America was practically settled"; the faith expressed by countless others through our history. That faith must begin with the teacher in the classroom. It must be at the center of our daily work, as well as of our long dreams. It must inspire us as both a personal and professional crusade for American youth.

Chapter II

THE CRISIS IN HIGHER EDUCATION

A guideline to the assessment of the role of higher education in dealing with the changes which now confront us, and those which are in the making, is the theme expressed in the opening statement of the report of the President's Committee on Education Beyond the High School.

"Revolutionary changes are occurring in American education of which even yet we are only dimly aware. This Nation has been propelled into a challenging new educational era since World War II by the convergence of powerful forces — an explosion of knowledge and population, a burst of technological and economic advance, the outbreak of ideological conflict and the uprooting of old political and cultural patterns on a worldwide scale, and an unparalleled demand by Americans for more and better education.

"These forces have created enormously increased educational challenges of which we have not yet taken full stock and which our educational institutions as a whole are ill-prepared to meet.

The gap between this Nation's educational needs and its educational effort is widening ominously."[1]

A revolution can be orderly, or it will be disruptive, in proportion to the degree to which its explosive forces are controlled. It is our task in the decade ahead to relate educational organization and practice to the explosions now in the making. These have been identified by President C. W. de Kiewiet of the University of Rochester as the explosion of knowledge, the explosion of the birth rate, and the explosion of "demand for the people whose function it is to apply knowledge to the conditions of human life."[2]

THE EXPLOSION OF NEW KNOWLEDGE

New knowledge is accumulated in a volume and at a rate scarcely to be comprehended. Nothing that has happened in history prepares us for this phenomenon. "The changes which all men who are forty or more have lived through," says George Sarton, "are greater than all the changes of the past put together. The evolution witnessed by the last two generations was more rapid than that of many thousand years; . . ."[3]

It was once held conceivable that all of man's important knowledge could be encompassed in a single published form. The name, "encyclopodia," has its origin in the concept that there can be a well-defined cycle of knowledge. The ancient scholar, Pliny, analyzed some 2,000 ancient books, gathered together 20,000 claimed facts under a variety of headings. This great Latin work was published in 77 A.D. and remained a standard source of information for over 1,000 years. The Middle Ages produced several encyclopedic works of importance, but the form, organization, and total coverage were not much altered.

After the 17th century, encyclopedias grew in numbers and

changed greatly in form and in scope, but perhaps the greatest change was the recognition that all important knowledge could not really be encompassed in one cycle. Today an encyclopedia of one subject, such as organic chemistry, cannot pose to present the important knowledge on that fraction of the world's information, and in this simple illustration we have a quick view of the explosion of knowledge in modern times.[4]

Mr. Harold H. Smith has used the change in speed of human travel as a dramatic index to the change in knowledge in our time.[5] He points out that from "the beginning of human evolution until the 19th Century, man was held to speeds of less than 40 miles per hour." This limitation was broken first by the steam locomotive in 1829, then by the automobile in 1910, then by the airplane. Now jets and missiles are practicable. A piloted aircraft has already traveled in level flight at 1,600 miles per hour.

This is a staggering achievement, points out Mr. Smith. It took 500,000 years to make a gain of 25 miles per hour and only 15 years to make a gain of nearly 300 miles per hour. "To consider that this represents only technological advance is to miss the whole spirit of human imagination and understanding. To be sure, the index is speed, but the real adventure is in the increased knowledge of aerodynamics, knowledge of combustion, knowledge of metals; knowledge of control of the world we live in. The same could be said today of any area of the basic sciences or developmental improvements dependent upon them."[6] And while this kind of dramatic measure is not applicable to all fields of knowledge, certainly the weight of expansion of things to be learned is going forward at an ever faster tempo.

The editor of *The Saturday Review* has summed up the challenge to education in the question, how to get it all in. "How to maintain certain values and approaches that have proved themselves through 160 years of public education and yet enable the individual to feel at home in the middle of a century which has already seen more change than has been accumulated in the previous 1000 years," is the key question to our curriculum makers today.[7]

What is the best education for changing times? How does one best give a student methodology for new knowledge along with memory of old? As even more changes are pending in the next 25 years, what should be the curriculum? Can we find the methodology for more effective instruction in the use of basic tools for the creation of attitudes that will make men and women equal to the new demands?

THE EXPLOSION IN POPULATION

When we come to a consideration of the explosions in population, we have another view of the role of higher education in the twentieth century.

Demographers have forecast additional millions in our population in the next half century, and other experts have outlined the demands which will come upon all of our common services, water supply, communication, transportation, and power. They have dwelt upon the heightened production of consumer goods and the need for more stores, shops, homes, apartments, garages. The implications for agriculture have been assessed and for the search for new materials, new processes, new production goals. Virtually every area of our economy is analyzing the significance of a rapidly mounting population.

The new population can mean increased prosperity. Prosperity creates additional demand for educational service and for an improvement in quality. Thus, the demand for educational service probably will increase at a higher rate than the population itself.

The requirements of the economy for continuing prosperity

will point up four questions basic in the supply of educational service:

1. How to take care of the new numbers?

2. How to retain for a longer period of membership those who do attend? In other words, how to reduce the drop-out proportion in the secondary school and the college?

3. How to induce students with ability who do not now enrol in post-high school work to do so?*

4. How to provide for adults' need for continuing education? The need for greater productivity will require that we bring into a high level of service those persons of ability who through lack of education or training are working at levels of productiveness below their potential.

From the continuing prosperity of the country, then, there will be two major influences upon education. At the same time that the arithmetic of the population increase presents an increased load, there will be a greater demand for service by a greater proportion of the people and a demand for an improved quality of education. On the other hand, the economic necessities will be such that the education of these numbers will not be adequate for the needs of the nation, so still further efforts will have to be made to recruit and retain a higher proportion in advanced schooling and in continuing education.

The practical problem arising from these demands will be confronted at the secondary school level and the collegiate level

---

* On this point, it is clear that financial need of students is not the sole controlling factor. All who have had experience with scholarship programs recognize that there are many elements other than financial ability which influence the decision to go on to school. The cultural pattern of the family is probably as important as economic resources. This statement does not minimize the importance of scholarships. It does suggest we should not depend upon scholarship programs alone to change the cultural pattern of American families. Some additional approach must be found to motivate able young people to go on to school.

and in ways of service not now covered by formal school agencies. The pressures on the elementary school, according to Dr. Dudley Kirk, will level off after 1960, but they will continue on the secondary schools and higher education until and beyond 1970 for reasons beyond the population increase.

EXPLOSION IN DEMAND FOR SPECIALISTS

Growing from the explosion in population and the explosion in new knowledge has come the demand for more expertly trained people to carry out the specialized tasks. Present shortages of specialized personnel have resulted in conspicuous raiding from one region to another, from one profession to another, from one institution to another.

Fighting the lag between what is known and what is practiced is a primary challenge in every field. And the forecast for the future is not reassuring.

Dr. Peter Drucker, in his analysis of America's next twenty years (*Harper's,* March through June, 1955), says that automation will bring a demand for "incredibly large numbers of men . . . in new highly skilled jobs." In addition, "large numbers of highly educated men will be needed in new jobs as designers of machinery, draftsmen, system engineers, mathematicians or logicians. Finally, enlarged numbers will be needed for new managerial jobs requiring a high ability to think, to analyse, to make decisions, and to assume risks."

"Mass production upgraded the unskilled laborer of yesterday into the semi-skilled machine operator of today. . . . In just the same way, Automation will upgrade the semi-skilled machine operator of today into a highly skilled and knowledgeable technician. . . ." Continuing, Dr. Drucker says, "The really serious social problem is not employment but the need to upgrade whole segments of the population in a very short time. Automation requires trained and educated people in unprecedented num-bers. The quantitative need alone will be so great that the eight or ten million college students we can expect fifteen years hence will be barely sufficient. One large manufacturing com-pany (now employing 150,000) figures that it will need *seven thousand* college graduates a year, once it is automated, just to keep going; today it hires three hundred annually."

"But the need is above all qualitative — for *better educated* people . . . the man who has acquired high gadgeteering skill will not do. Even in routine jobs, Automation will require abil-ity to think, a trained imagination, and good judgment, plus some skill in logical methods, some mathematical understanding, and some ability well above the elementary level to read and write — in a word the normal equipment of educated people."

In summary, then, there will be an increase in educational demand beyond the arithmetical increase in population, and the economic necessity for more and highly trained people is assur-ance that the physical task will somehow get done. These are the outcomes of prosperity linked with population increase. But the question now before the American people is "Will the job get done in time?"

THE NEED FOR QUALITY

Any college or university looking to the future must place its opportunity against the need to harness the power of these three explosions, the explosions of new knowledge, of people and of the demand for the product of the colleges.

Here it may be observed that we have not yet come to an understanding of the meaning of the numbers. They are statis-tics and we have not translated the statistics into human terms. The time is late in our coming to grips with proposed solutions. It takes four years to build a building — from idea through fund raising, planning and construction. It takes from six to ten years to produce a teacher.

Many are concerned that the new numbers will reduce quality. Quality is endangered when we do not have the resources or methods for an enlarged task. The danger to quality lies in our not getting ready rapidly enough for the new tasks.

We shall have to increase the case load in every professional service, and to learn to do this without burdening the worker, without lessening the force of the contact with the individual and without sacrificing quality.

The physical needs for education will somehow be met. It is not as clear how the teaching task will get done.

Central to the consideration of every problem related to educational service is the terrific expectation of the teacher. Whether the objective be improvement in mental hygiene, physical fitness, vocational guidance, or inspiration for a teaching career, the discussion turns to what the teacher can do about it! The recruitment, preparation, retention, inspiration and growth of teachers are central to any view of education in the next twenty-five years.

There are many questions to be answered, but the basic one, which will continuously confront the American people, is: What is the public purpose of education? Do we believe in its social benefits, and are we, therefore, willing to ask society to pay for it through philanthropy and taxation?

Do we believe in the economic inter-relationship of educational performance and economic growth, in the relationship of education to the improvement of the public health and the maintenance of the professions, in the improvement of public welfare, including national defense, and in the contribution of education to the morale of our people in the conservation of the individual's freedom and opportunity for growth? If we do, we shall resist the raising of economic barriers to educational opportunity which accompany increased charges to students.

If our answer is "Yes" to these questions, we must be committed to carrying out these purposes, stretching ourselves in gifts and in taxes for their support. Education will not be supported adequately until the questions are answered affirmatively. Difficult decisions will have to be made, purposes will have to be defined, priorities will have to be established.

If it is true that "what happens to American education will happen to America," the deficits in dollars, teachers, classrooms, and services in meeting the load of today, without considering the new numbers of tomorrow, mark out a national concern as serious as how to defend ourselves in a world of international tension. For we shall not be able to defend ourselves effectively unless we depend upon brain power more than manpower, upon new ideas more than arsenals, upon the morale of the people more than regimentation, upon economic strength more than diplomacy.

"In view of its unmistakable social utility, and what ought to be its pervasiveness in the lives of individuals, it is incongruous that education should be regarded as a special problem on the American scene. It is, rather, the base from which all important problems are to be attacked.

"The general failure to grasp this crucial distinction is evident in the nature of the inadequate commitment of American society to education."[8]

Chapter III

IMPLICATIONS FOR CAMPUS PLANNING

In the current discussion of the need for educational development, there is an increasing number who recognize that "education as usual" is not enough. To meet the requirements in basic research, in specialized personnel and in civic leadership — for the maintenance of prosperity and the building of effective national security — higher education must grow, in scope and in quality, at an accelerated rate.

Unfortunately, in Congress, in editorials, in many places of public discussion, the carefully studied measures proposed during the past five years have been too largely unheeded. The air is filled with unsound and unwise schemes and proposals. Old prejudices and nostrums are given a space age label and presented as quick and sure cures. Even more dangerous is the irresponsible and unsubstantiated criticism of education which produces no suggestion for improvement but breeds a lack of confidence in what now is being done.

It must be assumed that informed and devoted boards of trustees of our institutions are just as interested as any other agent or organization and usually more competent to make judgments about the efficiency of the internal operation of the institutions under their view. New organizations in the field of state planning can turn their attention much more profitably to the solution of those problems which no single institution can undertake alone. Data on per student costs, faculty loads, and student stations, are meaningless unless related to institutional purposes and quality. Consultants can help an institution in its self appraisal but real help comes from internal soul-searching not from irrelevant standards or comparisons.

At the same time it must be said that we shall not make as much progress as we should in state or regional planning, unless the spirit of inquiry is upon the individual institutions. Complacency and tradition on the part of any one member will inhibit or reduce group activity.

Without planning, an institution accumulates new activities and new programs haphazardly. Reference to wisely arranged priorities or even to well defined proprieties is impossible. Since all programs cannot be advanced simultaneously, a highly desirable move which causes a tolerable temporary imbalance may bring a very undesirable permanent imbalance, unless changes are sought within a design of institutional objectives.

Intramural planning, then, is a main concern of any institution trying to relate itself to the obligations and opportunities of these times, and is a condition of progressive or effective inter-institutional planning on a state or regional basis.

A first concern in such planning, should be improved operational efficiency. Education, like other enterprises, may be expected to improve from year to year. To meet a doubled load we obviously cannot expect to multiply by two just what we are doing now. Some choices will have to be made, and these involve choices at the departmental level. Numbers of courses, class sizes, plant utilization, teaching methods, organizational procedures must have the continuing appraisal of the faculty.

Assuming a clear understanding of objectives within the institution, by departments and colleges as well as for the whole, and assuming a continuing and wholehearted widely shared effort for improvement in operational efficiency, here are some of the topics which are currently receiving attention in vital and vigorous institutional self-study:

How may articulation be improved — between high school and college, between college and college within an institution, between curriculum and curriculum, between faculty and faculty, between the institution and its students, between the institution and its constituency, between the professional college and the profession?

How may General Education be given the nourishment and cultivation it requires in the midst of university specialization?

How may quality be increased without narrowing breadth of service?

How may the liberal arts be conserved, strengthened and extended in practice as well as in creed?

What new measures should be taken for the retention of able students?

How may superior students be identified and their work enriched or accelerated?

What is being done to recruit college teachers, for the profession in general as well as for immediate employment?

What kind of experimentation is underway for improving the teaching process and student learning? Are television, honors courses, library usage, lecture systems being studied for improved results?

What is being done to train the good alumnus and to develop future citizen interest in higher education?

What can be done to improve use of physical plant?

Both in teaching and research, how may interdisciplinary cooperation be developed?

How can the intellectual climate of the campus be improved, beyond the conventional academic activities?

What is the measure of resources needed, in physical plant and
operational finance, to carry out the institutional objectives during
the next ten years?

While the recent fashion for institutional self-studies across
the land is to be commended, it is also to be noted that the
questions involved in the self-study are those with which an
institution ought to be dealing on a continuing basis. New spurts
of interest in the subject are not likely to be productive of permanent results. In the same vein, it is futile to expect creative
results in state planning unless the same spirit of inquiry, professional analysis and objective deliberation is present within the
institutions which seek to plan together.

The Educational Policies Commission supports the point that
external coordination is dependent upon the action of the individual institution. Thus, it is essential that the internal organization "be set up in ways to use all its human resources. Within
the college all its members are important to the evolution of
policy. With the president as a coordinating agent, the faculty
as custodians of the scholarly tradition, students increasingly
responsible to the institution which nurtures them, and boards of
trustees representing the public interest and charged with ultimate decision on policy proposals — the individual institution
remains the heart of the American system."[1]

On the need to examine internal operations, Chancellor
Samuel Gould has made an arresting statement: "Paradoxical
as it may seem, I am convinced that the tremendous and terrify-
ing problems which suddenly face higher education in America
are fortunate: they make it mandatory for us to examine what

we are doing — to reassess our educational philosophy; to adopt new methods and adapt old ones; to find new resources in teachers, facilities and financing; and in general to play havoc with the *status quo*. We shall have to solve these problems or higher education will make a steadily decreasing contribution to the welfare of the nation, especially in the quality of its graduates."[2]

While it is true that the settlement of many of these issues will be beyond the control of any one university, no one institution is absolved from making its contribution to a professional solution of the questions raised. Someone has said that the cynic is the termite of education. This may be true, but I believe institutional lassitude in general professional matters is a far more serious threat to accelerated progress.

Chapter IV

IMPLICATIONS FOR RESEARCH

The American people may be said to be research-minded. The average person is impressed by research data, and many advertisements of new products lean heavily upon statistical reporting. "Progress is our most important product," with research illustrations, is the theme used to create institutional good will by one major American business organization.

Along with a ready acceptance of the values of research to business and industry, people have great expectations from research in medicine and in public health. The "miracle" drugs have raised the hopes of millions for improved prevention and cure of disease. New techniques in surgery, the development of antibiotics and new vaccines, the almost unbelievable discoveries of help for specific illnesses — such as polio, cholera, typhus — these facts of science and scientific achievement are deep in the consciousness of people everywhere, and they induce favorable attitudes toward research.

In still another area, popular ideas encourage support of research. Even if talk of a "push-button" war seems fantastic, we are building our national defense so that we may compete with space rockets and intercontinental missiles. Science, invention, and research have become the chief instruments of national security, and people not only take this point for granted but insist upon progress to an almost unreasonable degree.

Closer to everyday living, the benefits of research in the economy of our cities and states are assumed. The prevention of diseases among plants, the formulae for increased production from our soil, the industrial uses of agricultural products, the methods of the distribution system for products of all kinds, highway safety, new procedures for organization and management — almost every subject which has a bearing upon our health, safety, productivity, prosperity, is related to research activity, past and present.

The search for the new and the adaptation of the old has been the key to the dynamics of American national growth.

A demonstration of what has happened in research expansion may be seen in the statistics describing expenditures in industrial research.

According to the United States Department of Commerce, industry spending on research and development activities expanded from $430 million in 1945 to $4.25 billion in 1957. The expenditures from both government and business are estimated today to be in the neighborhood of $10 billion.[1]

The increase is even more dramatic over a thirty-year span. Thirty years ago our national spending on research and development was $170 million or two-tenths of 1 percent of a gross national product of $91 billion. In 1957 we spent 2.3 percent of the gross national product of $434 billion (or $10 billion) for these purposes.[2]

Apart from these impressive statistics, from our own personal experience we may recall that twenty years ago industrial research was a marginal operation in most companies. A. H. Raskin, of the *New York Times* has observed that

in only a few was there any systematic assault on the frontiers of knowledge; research departments were tucked away in corners of factories; funds and facilities for long-term studies were rarely available; complex assignments were farmed out to colleges or universities. Where large numbers of engineers were kept for development work, they often sat in regimented ranks in block-long lofts. Today industrial research is conducted in centers that have more kinship to a graduate campus than to an industrial plant. Bright young Ph.D.'s in physics, chemistry and mathematics hold skull-sessions with seasoned colleagues. Abstruse figures are drawn on blackboards. Ideas fly through the pipe smoke. Atom smashers, spectrometers, electron microscopes, computers, furnaces — all of these are to be found in corporate laboratories.[3]

To illustrate his description, Mr. Raskin cites the impressive technical center at General Motors, with its 320-acre campus and its twenty-five buildings, and the huge laboratories maintained by the General Electric and the Bell Telephone Companies. Mr. Raskin also cites the United States Steel program as illustrative of the new trend.

While all of this growth in research and development is impressive, one weakness must be corrected if the past trends of industrial and economic growth are to continue. The proportion of effort and finance going into so-called basic research is insufficient.

I do not believe there is much point in debating the question of which is more important, basic or applied research. Often the distinguishing line is hard to find. Many times so-called basic research originates in the observations in short-range projects. When it is acknowledged that application is as important as the original idea in any new development and that the original idea is useless without application, an argument concerning which is more important is meaningless. The reverse is also true: without new basic ideas, applications will be limited. This is true in science, in engineering, in public health, in the social sciences, even in the humanities and in the arts.

Accepting the thesis that basic research is a part of the whole of progress in research and development, we have cause to be concerned about the present proportions of the several parts.

While the total sums spent on research and development have increased many times in thirty years, the percent for basic research has declined from 20 to 10 percent of the whole.[4]

Why is this fact ominous? According to Professor N. J. Berrill of McGill University, present-day science is an enormous superstructure resting on deeply sunken pillars, representing the work of individuals.[5] Nothing was further from the minds of a small group of atomic physicists of the 1930's than the release of atomic energy for nuclear war.

To illustrate the point, President Norman Auburn of the University of Akron recently asked, how much longer can we rely on the know-how and inventive genius of the European scientists? "We well remember that we are indebted to German, Italian and Danish scientists for the development of the atom bomb, and more recently of rockets and missiles. Where would we be today if Wernher von Braun, Edward Teller or Ernest Steinhoff had decided to settle in another country? Where would we be if the Army's "Operation Paperclip," designed to bring West European scientists to this country, had failed?"[6]

Accepting the judgment of the students and observers of science progress in this country that basic research is the foundation for all research and development and that we are deficient in the scope and support of basic research in industry and government, I come to another point of concern which should influence our priorities of attention: the role of our colleges and universities in basic research.

"Much of the basic research, historically, has been undertaken on the university campus. This research, so valuable in developing new products and processes, must be maintained if the future progress of both society and industry is to be promoted adequately."[7]

The university has three contributions to make to the research of the nation. First, it trains the men and women who fill the positions in business and industrial research and who become the teachers of scientists and research workers. Second, in the teaching process, the university develops research outcomes which contribute to the bank of ideas for future development. Third, the faculties constitute a pool of advisory and consultative talent for business and industrial life.

The men and women in our colleges and universities who train others to do research and who themselves perform research are one of the vital resources of the nation. In a recent report of the American Council of Learned Societies, we have this statement:

Behind all . . . men of affairs, whether they realize it or not, stands the work of a relatively small number of scholars. If these are in short supply, the research which produces new ideas and new understanding will decline, but the funds now available for basic research in this country are minute in comparison to the amounts devoted to exploiting its applications. This is as true in science as in the social sciences and humanities. If those who are capable of advancing the frontiers of knowledge are supported only in their teaching and training of others, research will suffer and, eventually, teaching and training will suffer as well. It is not enough to transmit and apply our present store of learning.[8]

In measuring the future of higher education in America, there is a present danger that the research function of colleges and universities will be overlooked. The unrealized idea is not measured. The restricted opportunity is not felt. In the trend line of the future, however, they will be missed. Missiles and rockets would have been impossible without the scientific ideas which gave them birth. Cancer is being fought in the biochemistry laboratories; radio-astronomy has become an arm of space technology; in short, university research today is on the frontier of the new ideas in science, sociology, and engineering. Basic research is not alone identified with large organizations and huge installations. The individual teacher and student with an inquiring mind, at work in a campus laboratory, may also be the source of the new idea.

Today less than a hundred institutions in the country have comprehensive programs in basic research. Colleges and universities do about half the basic research in this country, in dollar terms, and considerably more than half in terms of work performed. About 97 percent of all research (in terms of dollars) in colleges and universities is done in 173 of the larger institutions.[9] Over one-half of the Ph.D.'s of the nation are awarded by the 93 land-grant colleges and state universities.

President Pusey of Harvard has pointed out that probably nine out of every ten major books of chemistry, physics, or biology, at every level, come from universities. "Thus despite the tremendous growth of American industrial research it is the university which also plays the major role in generalizing, synthesizing and disseminating scientific knowledge."[10]

The formula of needs in university research is simple. The universities need space, they need men, and they need superior students. Many federal grants to the universities today, for example, take no account of the fact that the work will have to be done in laboratories which are often outmoded, outworn, and obsolete. Scholarships are granted for young people to work with professors who are underpaid. If the universities are to continue as important sources of basic research, their people must have a place to work, must have the equipment to do the job, must have superior students, and must have a standard of living comparable with that of their peers. These points are so elementary, they ought not to require mention; yet, there is not a university in the country which would certify that its needs in these regards are being adequately measured, let alone filled. Dr. James Killian, chairman of the Corporation of the Massachusetts Institute of Technology and former science adviser to the President of the United States, supports this point of view:

"We have a few centers of great distinction — as distinguished as any to be found in the world — but we have too few of these and only a handful that excel in more than one field of science. We need more top-flight graduate schools of science with more top-flight departments. We should have twice as many first-rate graduate schools of engineering as we now have. At the last count we were producing only about 650 doctor's degrees in engineering each year, and this is not enough."[11]

Since educated manpower and new knowledge are indispensable to the proper development of the business enterprise, says J. Whitney Bunting of General Electric, the present situation requires "a proper understanding of the role of graduate education in industrial and business progress and . . . a reevaluation of relations policies that may not presently reflect the true interest of business in higher education."[12]

What must be done to change the priorities, to emphasize the contribution of the universities to research activity in this country?

First, the total salary structure for the teaching profession must be strengthened, so that universities are competitive with other professions in holding the research scholar.

Second, more money must be spent for research activity. Legislatures must be encouraged to consider the research function on a par with the instruction function. Donors, corporate and individual, must be encouraged to give more money for research.

Third, research grants to universities should be less restricted, whether they come from the Federal Government, the state government, foundations, or industrial and business organizations.

The bulk of new support for research in recent years has been for specific projects, projects sharply defined, with objectives specifically limited. This approach has governed most of the new support that has come from government, foundations, and corporations. We are afflicted with "projectitis." The universities are being influenced to modify their historic role as centers of free inquiry to centers of inquiry on subjects for which they can get funds. There is nothing wrong with project research as long as adequate support is given to the scholar in his search for new knowledge wherever his instincts, interests, and abilities lead him rather than where the dollars he can get will permit him to go.

Fourth, gifts and grants for space and equipment and continuing expenses of the institution must be regarded as important as fellowships, prizes, and awards. The institution must have unrestricted help in meeting its total obligations and not be expected to carry the overhead of a project or grant.

Fifth, the place of the research teacher in society must be much more broadly understood if we are to attract to the profession the talented, able young men and women who will become the teachers of tomorrow.

Sixth, the relationship between the research function of higher education and business advancement must be given greater public display by business leaders and the interpreters of business activity. An example may be taken from data reported by the Association of American Railroads on "Research and Estimated Savings Resulting," showing that since 1914 the University of Illinois has received $891,000 for work in this field, and as a result railroads have saved $240 million with savings continuing at the rate of over $13 million each year. This is a 270-fold return on costs with a 140 percent continuing annual dividend.

In a recent report of a national commission, entitled *The Efficiency of Freedom,* we have the statement:

"It is important to recognize a principle implicit here: Institutions of higher learning . . . serve both the end of knowledge itself, without regard for its immediate necessity, and the practical needs of the community. Thus, the importance of the colleges and universities to society can hardly be overemphasized. Without continuing research and a steady outpouring of graduates from these schools, the scientific and humane achievements of American civilization would soon perish.[13]

From industrial production to national defense, from the cultural behavior of communities to the conservation of the public health, the basic work in training for research and in research achievement are the responsibility of a too small percentage of institutions. The number must be enlarged and those now carrying on must be strengthened.

The opportunities are so great in the future for research that "the outcomes should be measured," said Dr. W. O. Fenn of the University of Rochester, "in kiloman-centuries rather than man-hours. The far reaching effects of research tomorrow require a special kind of measure."[14] They also require a reappraisal of the priorities in our support, our attention, and our understanding.

Chapter V

IMPLICATIONS FOR THE "SERVICE" ROLE OF UNIVERSITIES

Education, Research and Service are the component elements of the University Program. Because Service is difficult to define or measure, to see in exact form, this aspect of the University's work has not had the emphasis and support equal to the other two. Furthermore, many nonclass teaching activities, such as clinics, have not been clearly identified in their academic nature. Now we are coming to see the unity of university performance, to recognize that research cannot be separated from teaching, and that neither of these can be viewed apart from service, the social applications of teaching and investigation.

SERVICE IN ADULT EDUCATION

The President's Committee on Education Beyond the High School made the point that "no longer is there a single 'American educational system.' Four major educational complexes have evolved — our traditional system of schools and colleges, an elaborate educational program under the military, a mushrooming system of education operated by private business for its own employees, and a great variety of programs of continuing education under the broad title of 'adult education'."[1]

In another place, the Report stated "Adult education is coming of age in America, although certain other countries caught the vision of its future many years earlier than we. In recent years its growth in the United States has been dramatic, as might be expected in a society which changes rapidly and which has increasing leisure time.

"As the pressures on educational resources increase, adult education programs will be substantially affected. The Committee fears that unless its potentials are more widely understood and accepted, its future more carefully planned, its aims more clearly defined, its programs better organized, and new approaches found for doing its job better, competition for scarce resources may deter adult education from the full realization of its potentials."[2]

One out of every three adults in the United States is engaged in some kind of continuing education in any one year. Rough estimates indicate that fifty million persons participated in programs of adult education in 1955. Approximately 2,800,000 people were contributing some or all of their time to these programs. In 1954 there were as many new enrolments in correspondence instruction as there were freshmen or new students in colleges and universities.

"The educational needs of these adults are met through the programs of University Extension, evening schools, cooperative agriculture extension, public schools, community colleges, educational radio and television, correspondence schools, volunteer organizations, churches, community centers"[3] and a host of other agencies. The enrolees seek these opportunities for a variety of reasons — the desire of mature people to qualify for occupational advancement, to fill gaps at any level of formal education or to enrich and to improve daily living — are but several. But whatever the motivation and the way in which educational fulfillment is sought, it is eminently clear that the dimensions of continuing education for adults are enormous and are growing daily.

All of this merely supports the point that adult education in a relatively short time within our memory has come from the periphery of education to a central place. We have always had, in the history of our country, a concept of the broadly educated citizenry. The faith of Thomas Jefferson in popular education found expression in the birth of the common school and in the establishment of colleges and academies in his time. But these were instruments for the education of the young. Even at the opening of the twentieth century, the adult who did not have the advantage of education while young might be personally inspired by the legend of Lincoln at the fireside or later he might use Eliot's Five-Foot shelf of books, but his continuing growth in educational ways had to be self-propelled with little institutional help or service.

Adult education really started with limited purposes, using the left over or makeshift tools of other educational service. The "Americanization" classes for the foreign-born in the early years of the century is an example. Another push came from the self-improvement courses of the correspondence schools; then the extension departments, the night schools and the evening colleges were started.

During the depression came the federally subsidized educational programs for adults, under WPA, ERA, and the CCC; and there were others. However we may appraise the immediate outcomes of these programs, they established two additional premises: first, the adult can and should be served through the local community; second, the adult is interested in education for leisure time, recreation, and personal enrichment, as well as for the other outcomes. Homemaking, child care, parent education, personal efficiency also come in for a great deal of attention in these new definitions.

At the same time that the concept of adult education was broadening and its purposes deepening, its tools fortunately were improving. Once the class in adult education was nothing more than a day school class at night using the same organization of material, often having the same teachers whose only motivation for employment was the extra pay. The same techniques that were used in the daytime for high schools or even elementary were used at night. It was inevitable, however, that adult education teachers should become identified as people who must have special skills in communication, in motivation, in the adaptation of materials to adult classes. It was inevitable that the formal class should change to a discussion group, and that we should find the workshop, the camp setting, the conference as effective devices. Informal education came to have a new meaning and to describe a new approach to the education of the adult.

This movement of adult education from the periphery of educational service to a central place is given perspective by Howard McClusky, of the University of Michigan, in these words: "Just as the Nineteenth Century witnessed the growth and acceptance of elementary education, and just as the first half and second quarter of the Twentieth Century have, respectively, embraced the development of secondary and higher education, so will the next fifty years see adult education come to full stature as a phase of an advancing and dynamic culture. It will be accepted without reservation as the fourth and culminating level of education." Whether or not one agrees with these words of Mr.

McClusky, the point is clear that adult education has come into a new place in the total picture of American educational service.

At the present moment many are concerned that the prospective enrolments confronting the colleges and universities may take so much time and attention and resources that the requirements for the other parts of the total university task will be overlooked. Our approach should be not to shut ourselves off from any one of these historic functions; rather, our task is to keep them in balance and to keep them well supported with resources for excellence.

The University has only a part of the Adult Education and Community Service obligation. It must be limited in what it does by the philosophy and purposes of the institution, and the available resources. Only in this way can the service function have full acceptance in the University family, an appropriate share of University resources, and an effective definition of mission. This approach distinguishes University activity from social service and from recreation, as such, from local elementary-secondary evening schools service, from corporation in-service training.

Under pressures of numbers, other demands, and limited resources, a University has to make choices. It cannot be all things to all people. The Service function must come within this measure. It must be related to the teaching and research objectives of the institution of which it is a part.

When thus integrated, the Service role of the University is a major instrument for the fulfilment of its over-all objectives.

To illustrate the point I cite two views from distinguished Americans, one a comment fifty years old and a second one given recently. The first comes from William Rainey Harper, the great pioneer president of the University of Chicago. "Some universities," he said in 1902, "are deaf to the cry of suffering humanity; some are exclusive and shut up in themselves; but the true university, the university of the future, is one, the motto of which will be: Service for mankind, wherever mankind is, whether within scholastic walls or without those walls and in the world at large."[4]

The message for the contemporary audience has been phrased by Mr. Henry Heald, President of the Ford Foundation: "The college or university today is not an island of culture in an intellectual wasteland, not a monastic retreat for bearded scholars, not a training ground for an educated elite, not a country club for a privileged few.

"Our colleges and universities have become servants of the people and ministers to the public welfare. Our nation has come to the point where every field of human endeavor, where, indeed, our progress and survival, depend upon educated people."[5]

SERVICE TO THE COMMUNITY

The role of institutional service must be seen in the community context as well as in the benefits of Adult Education to individuals.

An *enlightened* society begins at home — in those community organizations that make for personal enrichment, the libraries, the schools, the museums, the study groups, in the community concern for public health and improved living conditions, in cooperative efforts for economic stability and intergroup harmony.

Community responsibility, then, is both a means and an end of education. Educational services must be concerned with both achievements and failures at the community level.

Dean Schneider had this vision when, many years ago, he established the first "cooperative" education program, in the

University of Cincinnati. He said the urban university "should be so devised that all the truth it possesses shall surely reach into the kitchens of the tenements and into the councils of the greatest banks, into the dreariest job that ever a child goes to and into the power plants that carry him there. Whatever the people of the city do, whether it be in manufacture, commerce, education, transportation, housing, government, baking bread, or building bridges, there the truth shall be wrought into the working organism of the doing of it. This is the basic philosophy of the matter."[6]

Some deplore the broad scope and variety of the university program on the assumption that had its range not been so wide, more resources would have been available for what remained. I believe the opposite is true. A less far-flung enterprise would have made less impact upon the public welfare; fewer people would have been served; and it is fair to assume that instead of more resources having been available for a more limited program, as some suggest might have been true, proportionately fewer resources would have been provided.

Those who object to University extramural service would take the institution out of the main stream of American life. The educational needs of people transcend the neatly compartmentalized packages of curriculum planners. If we believe that education is central to individual growth and to the well-being of our civic and economic life, then the university will make every effort to extend its resources to all who can benefit from them. It accepts community service as a main-line responsibility and seeks directly to fill community needs in many ways.

The American community is of strategic concern in a world of tension, in this time of major decision on new national policies. The structure of democratic performance is, in large part, dependent upon the effectiveness of the local community organization. We can withstand the stress of partial state and national regimentation if the community foundation of our democracy is sturdy. We need not fear any threat to free inquiry and open-mindedness if we have the wholesome appraisal of neighbors at the community level. We can survive the contests of propaganda, waged by political forces, vested interests, partisan groups of all kinds, if the local community is organized for constructive appraisal, sustained group action, and is dedicated to civic morality. The local community is the conservator of our civil rights, the home of our education, the basis of our economic prosperity.

We do not know very much about the nature of the American community, what causes it to behave as it does, or how it can be altered. We know that at moments of crisis the community rises to heroic group action, be it flood or fire or assault. Between crises, however, the community is likely to be apathetic, amorphous, tolerant of horrible slum conditions, inadequate schools, serious delinquency.

At this strategic point, any agency that can bring constructive service to the American community should imaginatively do so and strongly be encouraged to do so.

The stimulation of communities for development and planning, the teaching of the techniques of problem solving, the encouragement of research as a tool in community development, the supplying of basic information from other sources are examples of areas of community service where a university is uniquely qualified to give leadership.

SERVICE, A VITAL DIMENSION

Samuel Gould has described with eloquence the message of academic community services: "It is my conviction," he said, "that a college in addition to its more readily accepted intellectual dimension which provides room for the highest kind of scholarship and training should have the dimension of community which offers a place for the general life enrichment of all who live nearby; young and old, artisan and farmer, and member of a profession, and college graduate, and the comparatively unschooled. Thus, many of the gaps of weaknesses which the new pressures of numbers are bound to create in formal education can be filled or strengthened as the college opens its doors and its resources to all in a friendly and informal fashion, without thought of credits or degrees or anything more than to assist the burgeoning of understanding in the individual as a member of a personal, physical, political, economic, artistic, and spiritual world. Out of this dimension can come the new strength for America. It can be born of a desire to make of each community a meeting place for ideas and fostered through the leadership of our educational institutions. It can create new and exciting uses for the great physical facilities and the intellectual and cultural resources which so many of our schools and colleges possess. Out of such a dimension can come a new unity of the people."[7]

Chapter VI

INSTITUTIONAL COOPERATION AND COORDINATION IN MEETING NEW RESPONSIBILITIES

Over the past four or five years, the public discussions of higher education have increasingly reflected a sense of urgency.

At first, the concern was over the developing shortages in specialized personnel in all fields of endeavor — law, the ministry, nursing, medicine, teaching — there were no exceptions.

Then the concern was directed to the ability of institutions to step up their student capacity as the implications of the population growth came to be understood. The feeling of urgency spread from the educators, planners, and employers to the parents of the young people for whom educational opportunity might be restricted.

Finally, reports of two presidential committees emphasized the danger not only to the national economy and public well-being, but to the national defense and the security of the country in international affairs, unless the whole of the educational system is immediately strengthened. Sputnik appeared as if to give an exclamation point to these warnings.

Now, at a time of increasing competition for the tax dollar and the philanthropic gift and at a time of increasing public worry over the level of public expenditure, America must determine the educational price for her standard of living and national security and how and in what way that price is to be paid.

As a result, the individual citizen is ambivalent in his attitude toward education.

On the one hand, he is amazed at the projected cost in dollars and energy to gear up the educational enterprise to the requirements of the space age.

On the other hand, he realizes that education has now become an instrument of national defense and international relations as well as of economic strength and individual fulfilment, and that he must support it adequately.

As he studies ways and means to strengthen education, we may be sure that he will expect wise planning, prudent management, efficient utilization of educational resources, by students and faculty alike, and a concern for improvement.

We may anticipate also that improved state planning will be a condition for improved public support. It will soon be obvious to all that a professional study of the need for higher education service in any area of the state with a careful measure of the potential contribution of all institutions will produce facts and perspective for a wise decision as to what should be done in supplying major needs. Further, among the public institutions particularly, it is clear that what is done in one geographical area should be related to a state policy to govern similar developments in other areas under comparable conditions.

At the same time that the need for improved coordination among institutions within a state or area is widely acknowledged, opinions usually differ widely as to how best to achieve that goal. A single board of control for the public institutions within a state is a way advocated by some, but experience with this device is uneven among the states where it has been tried and at best it cannot deal adequately with the institutions not within its jurisdiction. Further, merely amalgamating boards of control or creating a "super" board does not automatically achieve the result desired among the institutions directly concerned. There must also be carefully designed plans for integration of administration and of program and agreement on general objectives.

Coordination is a result, not a process. It cannot be imposed but is achieved only through careful cooperative planning. It does not arrive suddenly. Effective state plans grow out of the experience of institutions in working together. While machinery for consultation with all institutions is an imperative for true state planning, there is no simple method for the achievement of coordination. It will come only as we start working together on specific problems and with a common purpose.

Prerequisite even to a beginning in interinstitutional cooperation is a belief in the unity of educational welfare.

There has been too much discussion, in my opinion, about categories of institutions, public and private, large and small. Our concern ought to be in the totality of educational service and how best to help each one achieve its own purpose with the highest quality of performance.

We hear continuing reference to the "dual system" of higher education in America.

I believe the term is misleading. We have a multiple system. Among public institutions we have junior colleges, municipal four-year colleges and universities, regional state colleges, state limited purpose colleges, and state universities. Among privately controlled institutions, we have junior colleges, regional liberal arts colleges, special purpose colleges, urban universities, regional universities, and national universities. Within the small liberal arts college, public and private, we have those of compact liberal arts curriculum and those which have diversified vocational and professional preparation.

Too much emphasis has been given in recent times to the differences between public and private colleges, to the easy generalization that public institutions are all alike in nature and function while private ones are essentially different from them.

In the wide diversity of American higher education each institution has its part, and public and private institutions are more alike within their classification of function than they are unlike in their method of organization or source of support. Colleges are more accurately described in function and purpose than in source of support or composition of governing board.

If we have a division in higher education, it is regrettably between the strong and the weak, between institutions of quality and those unable to fulfil their potential. America has need of all and the day has come when no duality in quality should exist. Strengthening must come to all.

Henry Heald, President of the Ford Foundation, has emphasized the point in this way: "There are no special virtues attached to a university because of the nature of its support. The only criterion worthy of consideration is the quality of its program, and this means the intellectual ability of its students and faculty."[1]

Across the nation in the desperate efforts to build budgets and find resources for new tasks, there have occasionally developed tensions between institutions, sometimes between neighboring public institutions, sometimes between public and private institutions. Whenever such tensions exist, they have had their origin in limited understanding. They grow out of the mistaken notion that there is a single pot of money for education for which each institution must compete in a way that a larger share for one means less for someone else, or that there is a limited number of students to be shared.

As we look ahead, there is more to do than all put together will get done. There are enough resources to go around if higher education as a totality makes sufficient impact upon the public mind. Education is its own resource and as our free economy prospers from the fruits of education, increased nourishment will return to the source of the benefits, if the people understand the process. The welfare of higher education is indivisible. What helps one, helps all. What helps the group or hurts it, helps or hurts each one in some measure. Our competition as institutions is not with one another, but with public apathy and limited civic vision.

Education in our time requires the highest kind of statesmanship. Public statements of educators in responsible positions critical of other institutions generically or individually are not only in exceedingly bad taste, bordering on the unprofessional in unvalidated and unscholarly negative comment; but in confusing the public as to the needs and opportunities of institutions, the cause of higher education itself is weakened.

Institutions must be held accountable for their behavior. But criticism should be accurate, substantiated, and voiced with professional restraint and understanding. It is the immature or shortsighted who tears down another, thinking thereby to build up himself.

It is obvious that in the complex and extended business of higher education, there will be disagreements among individuals, among groups, and among institutions as to how best to get the job done. If each disagreement results in a charge of bad faith or of questionable motives, then obviously state planning will be taken out of the hands of the institutions and vested in other authorities. If, on the other hand, we can disagree among ourselves amicably, look forthrightly at all information, and bring an exchange of views to bear upon planning "before the fact," then there can be progress in cooperative planning.

Communication before new plans are inaugurated, when they affect other institutions, is essential to good faith and to the utilization of the ideas of others as to what is good for the state as a whole. Cooperative planning has shallow significance when advice is not sought at a time when it can be influential in the final decision. Basic to all cooperative planning is evidence of faith in mutual interest.

While each university must do its own work, fulfill its own opportunities, build its own strength, it should rejoice in the success of others. Society's needs are not bounded by the constituency or the region of an institution's service.

A "random approach" to public service "may have been sufficient when the need was far less complicated and urgent," says the Report of the President's Committee, "but it is wholly inadequate for the individual and social needs to today and tomorrow."[2]

In short, the new developments in planning, arising from citizen concern with the financial requirements and the effectiveness of education, to be productive must be based upon a broad view of higher education in the public service, upon facts rather than custom or bias, upon consultation rather than competition, and upon the ability to evolve adequate machinery for interinstitutional cooperation.

INTRAMURAL PLANNING

A time-wasting temptation confronts all initial efforts in state planning, namely, the attractiveness of probing into intramural business which has no bearing on interinstitutional development. There are some questions which can be resolved only by the institution itself, and general formulae about them lead to false generalization or unfortunate standardization.

A case in point is the effort to make interinstitutional comparisons on a dollar basis. There is no accounting analysis which gives an accurate representation of cost per student and there is no logical way that I know to give such a cost figure. It is easy enough to compute gross expenditure per student or net expenditure per student, but such figures have nothing to do with the actual cost per student. They are only indices to expenditures. Also, within the university costs obviously vary so greatly that an average estimated cost would be meaningless.

Further, even if we had a cost figure, it would have no meaning in relation to a comparable figure at other institutions, for no two institutions are exactly alike in scope, quality, objectives, setting or organization. Comparisons of costs among institutions are, therefore, not likely to be valid.

The same observation can be made about different programs within any one institution. Institutions should be appraised as to efficiency, effectiveness, and propriety of function, but these appraisals can be adequate only when they are pointed at internal evaluation. National or regional norms are sometimes helpful as guide lines, but here again comparisons are likely to be faulty.

It is appropriate, then, that we encourage internal appraisal and planning as a prelude to interinstitutional cooperation.

Conversely, however, in the growing complexity of educational affairs, improved communication between like-minded institutions with similar purposes and services or those bound together in other ways is of increasing importance to themselves as well as to their constituencies. It provides mutual stimulation, encourages internal appraisal, and makes possible appropriate joint action. Diversity need not make impossible either articulation or coordination by the voluntary process.

INTERINSTITUTIONAL PLANNING

What, then, are some of the topics which can best be approached in a cooperative consideration? What are some of the problems which can be solved only by joint action? What cooperative studies would be mutually helpful even when joint action is not involved — helpful to the individual institution, or to public understanding — or as a basis for over-all planning?

Articulation with the High Schools

High on the list of studies which would have immediate benefit to the institutions of a state would be a review of the current status of high school-university articulation and of the ways in which such articulation might be improved.

Determining what institutions could do in common — in testing, counseling and advising about admission practices in general — would bring significant savings in staff time and energy and lessen the confusion that now too often prevails among prospective students and some high school advisers.

Help to secondary schools in preparing students for college work may certainly be advanced more rapidly through the joint endeavor of the institutions of a state than through the miscellaneous activities of individual institutions.

General Questions on Enrolment and Service

Some general questions occur immediately to any agency or group dealing with state-wide planning in higher education. What are the trends in enrolments, interpreted, of course, in their relationship to economic conditions, employment opportunities, numbers of institutions, migration, and a host of other considerations familiar to the demographers? What kinds of new programs are needed and what new institutions, if any? How many professional colleges does the state need, in law, engineering, pharmacy, etc.? Where are branches of existing institutions needed? What is the role of the junior college in the state plan? Of technical institutes and specialized schools? How do plans of existing institutions relate to these questions? How is the probable procurement of facilities, faculty and finance related to these plans?

Charges to Students

While charges to students will vary among institutions, for a variety of historical and currently practical reasons, changes in the pattern of charges are of interest to neighboring institutions. Thus it is helpful for an institution to have available, in determining its own assessments, a study of current practices generally, impending changes and probable future developments.

Financial Aids to Students

Programs for financial aid to students are an admirable subject for joint planning. Loan funds and scholarship resources are uneven and inadequate when left to institutional development. More important, joint effort is proportionately more successful than accumulated individual efforts. The state-wide loan fund program in Massachusetts deserves wide observation. As the demand for loan funds increases, underwriting of collections can add resources not available to a single institution. State scholarship programs, under government or private auspices, are similarly enhanced when viewed on a state basis and built upon joint support and utilization.

Joint Use of Services

How may institutions cooperate in the joint use of services? Films, textbooks, library exchange, television, radio, visiting lectureships are examples of services and activities which are adaptable to joint use. Both savings in dollars and extension in coverage are possible by cooperative action in these areas.

Exchange of Curriculum Information

Formal exchange of information about curriculum development and organization and the courses involved would be mutually stimulating and enlarge the benefits that come now from haphazard and accidental professional communication.

Staff Recruitment

In the increasing competition for professional personnel, it might be useful for institutions to consider an agreement on practices to govern recruitment. At present, contracts are in effect unilateral, protecting only the individual, and often programs and services are at least temporarily harmed by the sudden departure of key personnel.

Cooperation in Special Areas

Confronted by an increasing demand for highly specialized research and instruction requiring enlarged specifications for personnel and facilities, voluntary allocation of responsibilities or joint enterprise, must be considered.

Certain large endeavors beyond the capacity of a single institution can succeed on an interinstitutional basis where there is a great common interest and a willingness to pool resources in its support. Moreover, such action often makes possible, by the very significance of the joint effort, the procurement of supplemental financial help, not otherwise available.

Unified Extension Service

With the rapid growth of adult education and the increasing

demand for educational service to adults, is a statewide unified extension service possible? Conservation of faculty, through employment from more institutions and reduction in present travel and simplification of administration, appear to be immediate benefits of such a plan.

Public Interpretation

Since public support is dependent upon public appreciation for the work of the colleges and universities, are there ways and means for institutions to work together for an improvement in public understanding of the total mission of higher education, the nature of institutions, and the reasons for broad support? The work of the President's Committee on Education Beyond the High School and of the correlated regional and state conferences has enlarged the awareness of the general nature and extent of the problems of higher education and their relationship to the general welfare. How may the interest thus generated, augmented by many other developments, be sustained and increased in an organized way at the state level?

Consultation in Institutional Expansion

The inauguration of a new major program or service of an institution or the extension of its work geographically, through branches or extension centers, inevitably has an impact upon the work of other institutions. Unilateral announcements, "after the fact," bring misunderstanding and sometimes ill will. More important, the action is often based upon inadequate planning as to what is good for the state as a whole or how the objective could be served in a better manner with a due regard to all institutional interests. No institution should regard what is best for the state as a whole as in any way inimical to its own sound institutional development. Machinery for interinstitutional consultation in the preliminary stages of planning for expansion is a basic requirement in state planning, both to minimize ill will between institutions and the resultant public confusion and to insure the best and most economical procedures for new developments.

Background Considerations

State planning is necessarily concerned with conservation, with improvement in present services, with economy and efficiency. But there are other questions equally important. How may the leadership of faculties be put to broader use in the life of the state? What services beyond teaching and beyond research can higher education provide which no other public service agency will undertake? How may the broad usefulness of our institutions be enhanced?

Machinery for State Planning

There is little advantage to talking about planning, however, and enumerating the agenda unless there is "brass tacks" thinking about the mechanism to bring institutions together for the purposes here outlined. Voluntary meetings will not suffice when general interest lags or when one or more members are indifferent or hostile. Machinery for debate, for communication, and for appraisal must be formally instituted and used.

Sometimes that machinery will be general in nature, with broad purposes, illustrated by the Illinois Commission of Higher Education. Sometimes it will be specialized, starting with one problem, or a few, but expecting to grow in scope and usefulness.

The important outcome of any consideration of this question is the creation of some continuing "ways and means" for joint consultation and action, however limited initially.

At this point it may be well to point out that while state planning may well begin with a state survey, it does not end there.

President J. Wayne Reitz of the University of Florida, in referring to "a rash of surveys at the state level of higher edu-

cation" called attention to their overemphasizing the quantitative aspects of institutional service, their failure to take into
account the informed evaluations of responsible administrators
and lay leaders, their search for simplified answers to the need
for coordination, with too much faith in "super-boards" and
super-imposed chancellors, their failure to take proper cogni-
zance of varying institutional objectives and responsibilities.[3]

In the end, the effectiveness of state planning rests with the
willingness of the individual institutions to participate and with
the desire on the part of each to work with others in the attack
on larger problems. Such willingness and desire will be expressed only when there is no threat, direct or indirect, to the
institution's autonomy or individuality, when there is no possibility of regimentation or political force. "The objective," says
the Educational Policies Commission, "should be maximum voluntary cooperation, arrived at by continuing study and supported by whatever framework of agreement is advantageous."[4]
All efforts at coordination, the *Report* continues, "must in the
end depend upon the action of individual institutions — action
based upon voluntary judgment, action designed to preserve the
individuality of the institution within the pattern of the whole
American enterprise."[5]

"Crash" programs will not work, however well intended. Talent search will be less than enough until the colleges and universities are strengthened in proportion to the measure of the
task they are called upon to perform.

As long as we harvest the talent of the nation from a broad
base, encourage its freedom of choice, and provide for adequate
educational opportunity, our national achievement will be adequate in the economic, scientific, or military competition of the
world.

State planning is essential cultivation in that harvest.

Chapter VII

THE ROLE OF THE FEDERAL GOVERNMENT IN HIGHER EDUCATION

In the summary of a discussion by the trustees of the Carnegie Foundation for the Advancement of Teaching in 1956 there is an arresting paragraph which provides an appropriate starting point for a consideration of the Federal Government and higher education.

The question at issue is not whether the federal government should have a role in higher education. That question was settled affirmatively in the nineteenth century and never seriously reopened. The question at issue is *what kind* of role the federal government should play in higher education. It is not a question about which either the American people or leaders in higher education are ever going to make a clear-cut decision. But they are going to make a great many decisions that bear in one way or another on federal action, and the cumulative impact of these decisions will determine the future of federal relationships to higher education. One can only hope that these decisions will be made with a clear grasp of the issues involved.[1]

61

THE GOVERNMENT'S PRESENT ROLE

According to Dean John C. Weaver of the University of Nebraska in a paper presented to the 1958 meeting of the Association of American Universities, federal expenditures on higher education have reached the proportion where the key question is not whether there should be such federal expenditures, but rather how are they to be spent and how are they to be expanded.

Present federal expenditures in the area of higher education reach a total of nearly $2 billion. Half of these appropriations goes to individuals, however, and the remainder (for research contracts and grants, medical research facilities, and special projects) is spread unevenly among the institutions and cannot in any sense be considered as helpful to institutions generally.

It is time that the Congress and the administration consider a proposal which will be of benefit to all institutions and still be within the responsibilities of the Federal Government.

The recently enacted National Defense Education Act of 1958 does not fully meet these specifications. Insofar as it touches higher education institutions, it is piecemeal, indirect, and uneven in its spread.

But generalized philosophical debate about federal aid for colleges and universities is fruitless. In the first place, what is often described under the heading of federal aid, either present or proposed, is not aid but either payment for services rendered or aid to individuals. Second, the debate is fruitless because programs of federal expenditures for higher education will not come in any over-all philosophical pattern.

In examining future federal financial participation in the costs of higher education, the issues are more meaningful, therefore, when appraised in the context of a specific plan. While it is proper that we analyze the merit of any proposal in terms of our philosophical premises, taking a strong, entrenched position on the other side of a doctrinaire battle over federal relationships is neither necessary nor helpful in the solution of the problems which confront higher education.

One of the reasons the Congress has not undertaken new programs of wide benefit to colleges and universities is that there has been no such program before the Congress which promised this effect and which has been widely supported by all important elements in higher education.

In the absence of a plan and in the confusion over what ought to be done, Congress has taken both limited and disappointing actions. For example, Congress in 1958 appropriated new millions of dollars to help encourage additional students to go to college. Its action brings to nearly $1 billion a year the amount payable to individuals to help them take specialized training or attend college in a general program.[2] These sums were appropriated to help students go to college at a time when unprecedented enrolments are already in prospect. Further, these actions were taken when there were before the Congress important measures to help the colleges handle the new numbers. The bills for loans for college housing, for payment for ROTC facilities, for administrative costs in public health research, for medical education teaching facilities, are examples of ways the Federal Government could appropriately have helped institutions and which should have had priority over the new appropriations which were authorized.

A piecemeal and inadequate Federal Government approach to the over-all needs of higher education will persist until there is a clear recognition of the national need and a definite proposal to help with answering that need on a wide front. Historically, the Federal Government has many times appropriated funds to help with causes, whether through public or private agencies, when the national welfare has been involved and a satisfactory formula was found. In the long history of federal grants, the precedents are ample for aiding institutions and organizations, whether public or private, which are operating in the national welfare. Subsidies to agriculture, to transportation, to hospitals, to highways are examples.

FINANCIAL BACKGROUND

Volumes have been written in the past five years on the general need of higher education for greatly expanded support.

Mr. Seymour E. Harris of Harvard University has suggested that the educational and general budget is going to rise from $3 billion to $9 billion in ten or twelve years. Whether one accepts Professor Harris' projection or his proposed solution, one must agree with his point that unorthodox methods of financing higher education must be considered.[3]

The issue was recently phrased quite clearly by Director Alan T. Waterman of the National Science Foundation in a statement prepared by him and approved by the National Science Foundation board: ". . . We must progress in our science and technology and in the education and training of our citizens with all the effectiveness and thoroughness we can muster. We cannot afford to delay in arguments as to how we do them. . . . We appear to forget that as a Nation we live in a competitive world and shall continue to do so. It seems abundantly clear that we shall rapidly lose in competition, unless we can show more determined and constructive efforts than we have during the past years."[4]

The Report of the President's Committee on Education Beyond the High School

It has been disappointing to many that the recommendations on federal finance of the President's Committee on Education Beyond the High School did not have formal consideration by the Congress. The legislative measures adopted were pretty largely outside the framework of the report of the President's Committee.

The Committee recommendations for federal action in the field of financing higher education were four in number. They still deserve consideration: (1) a continuation of federal loans for revenue-producing facilities; (2) payment of full costs of research and service contracts with institutions; (3) grants-in-aid for slum clearance where educational institutions were involved; (4) a program of grants for construction of academic buildings.

The first three have had limited debate and some action. The fourth has had little consideration by the Congress.

The report said: "A system of outright Federal grants on a matching basis to nonprofit educational institutions should be worked out. A system which might be adapted to this purpose has for some years provided assistance in the construction of medical hospitals, under the Hill-Burton Act. The provision for matching would be important, in order that State and private efforts be stimulated rather than retarded, and priority should probably be given to institutions seeking to expand their enrollments. It is hoped that ways may be found to extend the benefits of such a program to all types of nonprofit institutions of higher education; but in any event such aid should be extended to as large a proportion of the total number as possible."[5]

The Committee gave three reasons for assistance by the Federal Government in meeting construction costs. They were: "It would help institutions to concentrate more on financing adequate faculties. It can be terminated when enrolments level off, without disrupting institutions' current finances. It contains little if any possibility of Federal control of educational programs."[6]

The President's Committee report also pointed out: "Colleges and universities are now spending about three-quarters of a billion dollars annually on new facilities and modernization of old ones. Their capital outlay requirement for these purposes is estimated to be approximately $1.3 billion each year from now through 1970. There are already substantial deficiencies, although the really sharp increases in enrollment have not yet come."[7]

The recent study by the American Council on Education, prepared by John D. Long with others, has increased the amount, stating that the aggregate estimates of need for minimum adequacy run from a high of about $15 billion to a low of $12 billion.[8] Professor Long tells us that this forecast checks with the aggregate estimates developed through state projections.

E. V. Hollis of the U.S. Office of Education tells us that plant expansion needs alone justify the $12 billion estimate. A similar amount is needed to replace temporary and wholly obsolete buildings, he says; and $8 billion is needed for equipment, for land, site development, and utilities — or a total capital need in the next ten years of $33 billion.

Whichever of these estimates is accepted, the definition of need is far beyond present plans to cope with the problem.

Assuming that the obligation of the Federal Government for the total program in higher education is limited but also assuming that timely federal action is urgently needed to encourage local action, both public and private education might well unite in support of the recommendations of the President's Committee on Education Beyond the High School as a common ground for immediate progress.

This point of view was recently given encouragement by President Nathan Pusey of Harvard when he said: ". . . The National Science Foundation, the National Institutes of Health, the military services, the Atomic Energy Commission and other agencies are already contributing to specific ends of higher education. . . . Government is not the final solution to all our problems, but it is surely true that public funds — federal as well as state — must be brought to bear on our critical financial problem."[9]

I share the view that private institutions must receive some form of public support, if we are going to maintain a first-rate system of higher education, widely accessible to all able students, with the research and service roles strong. It is also clear that on a national base the states collectively are not moving rapidly enough to meet the cumulative needs of the public institutions.

A FEDERAL GRANTS PROGRAM FOR CONSTRUCTION OF ACADEMIC BUILDINGS

Dr. Alan Waterman has said: "The pressing problem for science and engineering in universities is to secure modern laboratories and research equipment, including rather costly equipment for the larger institutions, and to provide for large capital research facilities to be used nationally or at regional centers. In the interest of training future scientists, needs extend to undergraduate laboratories and demonstration equipment."[10]

Recognizing the national concern with science and engineering and realizing that science and engineering facilities constitute approximately one-half of the projected costs of building needs, it would be appropriate that implementing the recommendations of the President's Committee for construction grants be defined as related to science and engineering.

A federal building grants program, in the amount of $750 million a year for ten years, available to all institutions to match local capital funds for all purposes, including equipment, would materially increase the science and engineering education facilities of the nation. I repeat, the federal grants should match the local, not the reverse; and all capital expenditures made available at the local level should be counted in the pool of resources on the assumption that half would go to science and engineering laboratories and equipment.

Machinery for the definition of need could be established, comparable to that now in effect for making grants for the medical research facilities, if grants were made directly to institutions.

A plan comparable to the Hill-Burton legislation for hospital construction could be followed if grants to the states is a preferred method. Federal lease of buildings to institutions could be arranged where there are technical restrictions to outright grants. This program would have the following advantages:

1. It would recognize that higher education is an instrument of national defense and economic strength and help the nation to work toward a first-rate system of higher education. It would put the kind of national value on higher education that now obtains for hospitals, highways, and medical research.

2. Relieved of the burden to provide all of the facilities needed in the next decade, colleges and universities could direct more resources into salaries and other operation costs.

3. Giving money for buildings eliminates any possibility of federal control of the operation of educational programs.

4. As to the participation of private institutions, the case would be based on the concept that these institutions are important to the nation, and that building "grants" would be a subsidy for the continuation of that service, just as federal grants formerly have been made to private organizations when necessity required such action.

5. The Federal Government has recently adopted a program of grants for graduate work and for increased aid to students.

It is time that attention be given to helping the institutions do their job.

In general support of this approach, let me quote again from the President's Committee report:

Under our system, sovereignty, and hence responsibility, is shared between the Federal Government and the several States. And these latter, along with private groups, have traditionally borne the primary responsibility for the education of our people.

Yet it is obvious that the Nation as a whole has a vital interest in the education of its people. The political system and national security, health and prosperity depend heavily upon it. Areas that fall behind are sure to impair the standards of other localities. This has been the basis for acceptance of Federal operations in matters of security and economic stability. The Federal Government has the authority and can mobilize the resources to promote and support education also. It has exercised that authority many times.[11]

Precedents for Grants to Private Institutions

Precedents in federal subsidy for private institutions are many. In the thirties, emergency education measures applied to private institutions. The Surplus Property Act of 1944 applied to private institutions. The College Housing Loan provisions of the Housing Act of 1950 apply to private institutions. Construction grants for research facilities in medical, dental, and public health areas apply to private institutions.

A barrier to a clear view of federal grants to private institutions is not only the historical opposition of those who believe that public grants should be limited to publicly controlled agencies but also the difference of opinion among the private institutional spokesmen. Although some ask for federal tax exemption for educational expense as an indirect federal subsidy to private education, insofar as it would permit increased tuition, others refer to federal grants as if they were entirely inimical to educational integrity. The point of view of President Pusey previously quoted is an indication that leaders in private education will consider supporting a plan to implement the recommendation of the President's Committee.

Let us take a look at a parallel federal program. The Federal Hospital Survey and Construction Program, commonly known as the Hill-Burton Program, was signed into law in 1946. Between 1946 and July 1957, 35,000 projects at an estimated total cost of nearly $3 billion were undertaken. The federal contribution to this total was $809 million. The over-all program has added, or will add, more than 153,000 beds and 898 health units. Although 900,000 more hospital beds are needed, the effect of the Hill-Burton Program has been dramatic in getting this national need appraised and solutions devised.[12]

It is relevant to consider what the Federal Government is doing in the way of aid for highways.

Federal Aid Highway authorizations since World War II have provided federal funds for three classes of highways — primary, secondary and urban. A total of $550,000,000 was authorized for these three classes of highways for each of the fiscal years 1954 and 1955. Authorizations have steadily increased ever since to $700,-000,000 for 1956; $825,000,000 for 1957; $850,000,000 for 1958 and $875,000,000 for 1959. These funds are matched equally by the states.[13]

The 1958 Federal Aid for Highways authorized $900,000,000 for the fiscal year ending June 30, 1960 and $925,000,000 for the fiscal year ending June 30, 1961.[14]

Beginning with the fiscal year 1954, annual authorizations also have been made specifically for improvement of the national system of interstate and defense highways.

The Federal Aid Highway Act of 1956 inaugurated the long-range program for the intensive development of the interstate system authorizing a total of 24.825 billion dollars for the 13 fiscal years 1957-69 to provide for completion of the entire system. These funds are matched on a 90 percent Federal-10 percent state basis.[15]

And for those who think the projected building costs for colleges and universities are high, E. V. Hollis reminds us that capital expansion of industry and business annually is in excess of $30 billion.[16] Since 1947, $291 billion has been spent upon physical facilities by business.[17]

What is projected here ($7.5 billion in ten years) is a sum smaller than was appropriated by the Federal Government for the educational benefits to veterans, an amount which has reached a total of $14 billion.

In the context of other proposals, we may also make comparisons. Health, Education, and Welfare Secretary Arthur S. Flemming recently said that his advisory committee indicates the Federal Government should spend $0.5 billion a year on medical research (by 1970) and that his department, with others, should plan to fill this need.[18]

There are those who accept the propriety of and need for federal grants to private non-church-related institutions but who question the constitutionality of a plan to include sectarian institutions. They point out that support of federal grants for church-related hospitals and church-related medical schools (for research facilities) was based upon the rationalization — insofar as this issue is involved — that the services of hospitals and research laboratories of religious institutions are functions unrelated to religious purposes. This rationalization says that instruction even in medical schools and hospitals serves religious purposes whereas research and bedside service do not. In my view, this is a quibble.

In any event, the issue is too important to be resolved on what congressmen and others *think* is unconstitutional. Even constitutional lawyers are divided on the point. We shall not *know* the answer until a plan is adopted and tested in the courts. Grants to states is a mechanism which would place the religious issue at the state level. Leases of federal property to church-related colleges is another possibility. The grant distribution formulas used in Canada and Great Britain are worthy of study. Still other devices have been suggested.

Fear of unconstitutionality, as long as informed legal opinion is divided, should not be used as a barrier to action on a plan carefully designed to minimize the risk of challenge on the religious issue.

If later, by court decision, church-related colleges and universities are excluded from federal grants, at least other private institutions, along with the public, can be given assistance in meeting their potential to contribute to the national welfare.

In conclusion, I quote again from the Carnegie report:

It is not necessary to take a strong, entrenched position on either side of this doctrinal battle. A clear grasp of the issues leads one to accept certain arguments from both sides. American higher education *is* in desperate straits with respect to its financial future. This *is* a matter of national importance. If it is to be solved, all of the groups which have an interest in solving it must play an appropriate part. A healthy pattern of financing will involve contributions from many sources — students, alumni, the states, the federal government, business corporations, and philanthropic sources.[19]

Those who fear an increased federal grants program out of a general concern about expansion of federal responsibilities may be interested in the point of view of Marion B. Folsom, formerly Secretary of Health, Education, and Welfare:

An increase in government activity is not necessarily evil in itself — the central question is whether the government activity actually provides a needed and constructive service for the people. The *absence* of wise and prudent government action can be more costly in the long run. Sumner Slichter of Harvard has spoken persuasively on the theme that "government is not merely an expense — it is a service-rendering organization that repays its costs manyfold in the services that it renders."[20]

At a time of increasing competition for the tax dollar and the philanthropic gift, and at a time of increasing public concern at the level of public expenditure, citizens everywhere are confronted with the decision of how to pay the educational price for our standard of living and our national security, and how and in what way that price is to be paid. It is not enough that people applaud the idea of educational opportunity and educational standards of quality; it is essential that ways and means be found to pay for them. The key question confronting the American people is the extent to which new resources will be made available for the educational demands of the future.

Chapter VIII

HIGHER EDUCATION AND THE
AMERICAN PUBLIC

In measuring the positive and negative popular attitudes toward higher education, I believe the balance is overwhelmingly in support of the college and university system in the abstract. Of course, the public appraisal will reflect an occasional condescension toward the academic; a satirical note expressed in the terms "egg head" and "brain truster," and a welter of criticism based upon misconceptions of what college and university life is really like. While there is an uneasy awareness that colleges and universities face a financial crisis of major proportions, solutions are often suggested in easy generalizations about the number of students who ought not to attend college, or about the possibility of turning the stadium into a lecture hall. Statistics and abstractions are used without an assessment of the human values involved; and we hear misconceptions and half-truths bandied about as oversimplified panaceas for the needs that are becoming apparent, if not fully appreciated.

The specialized nature of the educative function and of the organization of education are not generally recognized. Nearly everyone has had school experience, and he generalizes from this experience. He may not have been in a classroom since his own student days, but he does not hesitate to use the memory of that experience as a basis for appraisal of what goes on today. He is humble in his evaluation of his business occupation; he does not measure his doctor by his childhood memories, or his pastor by his adolescent recollections. Yet he does not hesitate to assume authoritative judgment on educational matters because he has once been to school. Obsolescence of opinions and facts should produce more humility than is apparent in discussions of educational matters. Even the education specialists express themselves in the current fashion. The teacher who would not ordinarily reason from illustration or reach a conclusion on the point of a single instance too often forms opinions on educational issues from a highly personalized and limited point of view. It appears to be a human failing to enjoy the luxury of arrogance of opinion where responsibility is not involved.

Part of our difficulty in attaining public understanding arises from the knowledge that education perennially has had an imbalance between its aspirations and realizations, has never had enough resources to fully accomplish its mission. And there is the feeling that the problems now talked about are more of the same, with the familiarity of an old refrain.

An example of the failure to understand the nature of the crisis is reflected in the congressional reaction to requests for adequate research funds for the Office of Education. In the Department of Health, Education, and Welfare, the Congress gave more money for health research than was asked but turned down requests for aid for medical education to train personnel who can intelligently and effectively do medical research. It drastically cut requests for research funds for the Office of Education, but gave the Atomic Energy Commission funds to underwrite an experiment in how to stimulate high school teachers to a greater interest in science.

THE GAP IN PUBLIC UNDERSTANDING

These inconsistencies in an appraisal of the nature and extent of the task confronting higher education are characteristic of the present public attitudes. But, in the abstract, there is a faith in higher education, a feeling for the importance of research and intellectual advancement, an admiration for things cultural and aesthetic, and an almost passionate advocacy of the right of youth to have an opportunity for an education commensurate with talent, a sense of the relationship between economic advancement and the education of people, between national defense and trained brainpower, between civic health and the preparation of leaders for public service.

There is a wide gap, however, between creed and practice, between faith and fulfillment, between appreciation and appropriate action.

HIGHER EDUCATION AND THE MASS MEDIA

The importance of an informed public opinion about the individual institution and higher education in general is now quite widely accepted among educators. The hostility toward the lay adviser has disappeared; the resentment of the journalistic interpretation of science is nearly gone; the isolation of the academic community is no longer celebrated as a major virtue.

How recent is this changed attitude is illustrated by the fact that it has been within the memory of most of us that formal institutional interpretation has been considered proper. It was not long ago that the first people especially assigned to the task were "borrowed" from the faculties in English and journalism, with a few unorthodox appointments from the professional ranks of journalists and related fields. There are instances today where major institutions are defensive about the interpretive effort and, because they fear misunderstanding about expenditures for public relations activities, fail to fulfill their responsibility to let the people know how and why and with what results their support is utilized.

From this relatively new sensitivity to the importance of public understanding, it has been natural for institutions to turn to the instruments of communication as quick help for improved relationships. Most institutions today are more or less organized for cooperation with newspapers, magazines, radio, and television. To a lesser extent they utilize film and rostrum, but the variations in use may be traced to lack of resources rather than desire.

In these recent years, the agencies of the so-called mass media have made an enormous contribution to the understanding of higher education. The steadily increasing proportion of youth of college age in attendance at our institutions is testimony to the increasing public acceptance of the values of higher education, and much of that favorable appraisal has derived from the interpretation of higher education in the press, the journals, and on radio and television.

Even with the friendliest of attitudes and the most sympathetic of intentions on the part of the directors of mass media, however, there are limitations as to what they can accomplish in creating public understanding and appreciation. While education deals with human problems, the business of education is not completely understood through the anecdote or the narrative, which are the essence of the human interest story. Features and news present parts, seldom the whole. That which is interesting or dramatic is not necessarily the most illuminating; and that which is known is not always fully comprehended. Public understanding of higher education must be sought in ways beyond the mass media. Education as a function and as a process is one of the most complex in modern society, and the most complex of those directly dependent upon lay appreciation.

There are twenty thousand vocations and professions which require some educational preparation. Concern with home life, social and civic life, and personal living on the highest terms is also the business of the schools and must be dealt with in realistic relationship to the wide range of individual interests, talents, and abilities.

How can such an enterprise be translated for, let alone evaluated by, the average citizen, whose money in gifts and taxes must support it, is the key question confronting higher education today. With all the help possible from friendly associates in the agencies of mass communication, the desired public understanding of the complex institutional task must go beyond the dissemination of information.

THE MUTUALITY OF PUBLIC RELATIONS AND LAY PARTICIPATION

Public relations in the broad sense only begin with the organization and dissemination of information about the institutional program. The determining factor in public appraisal is the adequacy of the program itself; and no institutional program will be as effective as it can be unless it is built upon a continuing concern with how best to adapt the program to the needs and aspirations of the society of which it is a part. Understanding is a two-way process. Efforts at improved relations will be superficial and justifiably suspect unless they are grounded in an honest effort to learn the desires and concerns of the other party.

Organized efforts to gain the understanding of educators of the vital purposes of other identifiable segments of the public have increased in number and are growing in effectiveness and acceptance. Many other forces outside of education have been at work to break the academic isolation of other days. However, these are germane to our present topic only in noting that the improvement in relationships with the public of higher education is a reciprocal process; and the reciprocity is under way. The appreciation of colleges and universities for such organized lay interest in higher education has developed during the past twenty years. Before World War I, academic communities were somewhat withdrawn from the life of every day, both for students and for faculty. The layman was tolerated in university life only when he was a potential benefactor, and the educator went to the layman only when he was in financial trouble and then in no organized way.

At the college and university level, considerable progress in citizen involvement has been made. Committees advisory to divisional programs and to institutions as a whole have been established. Governing boards have created organizations of associates. Acquaintanceship with local civic and professional organizations has been deepened and two-way communication improved. I believe that direct widespread lay participation in the consideration of educational problems is the only method by which the tremendously complicated work of the schools can achieve broad public understanding. However, such lay participation in institutional affairs will be superficial and ineffectual unless both parties regard the relationship as vital.

THE ESSENTIAL ROLE OF ALUMNI

What are the possibilities of alumni participating, effectively, in activating America's reappraisal of its purposes and priorities in higher education? To what extent can alumni help keep a state of transition in higher education from remaining a state of suspense?

In answering this question, we must take into account two views of the alumni body.

On the one hand we have the traditional estimate given by the late Chancellor Samuel Capen of Buffalo: "In the long run, the alumni of American universities are responsible for what each institution becomes. They constitute the dominant groups of citizens in these republics of letters. As such they hold the ultimate destinies of the universities in their hands."

Henry Heald has put it: "The ultimate continuing strength of a university rests with its alumni. . . . They are keepers of the tradition, preferred stockholders of the enterprise, the mark of its accomplishment."

On the other hand a look at alumni relations in institutions across the land reveals that we have been unable to build into student experience that filial affection and regard for alma mater which might reasonably be expected. Whether the measure be in memberships in alumni associations, in the record of gifts, in public opinions expressed, or in the initiative in support of university causes, the gap between those who may be counted upon and those who are indifferent is a wide one indeed. I do not say this to minimize in any way the tremendous contributions that have been made by those loyal and effective workers enlisted in the support of their institutions. That they are a minority, however, cannot be refuted, and that they are a much smaller minority than we might expect cannot be denied. The university that is fairly certain how to make a good chemist or physician or teacher is not at all certain, as the records will show, how to make a good alumnus.

In view of the decisions to be made on purposes and priorities in relationship to education, the extent of alumni participation may be crucial.

The alumnus has always been important to his college or university for support moral and material and as the witness of the university's achievements in human relations. Today he is more important than ever. As America searches its soul on the "how" of educational welfare, it needs the service of the alumnus — for reassurance, for stimulation, for encouragement, for counsel. If those who have been the direct beneficiaries of our system of higher education do not lead the way in seeking a meaningful national commitment, how can we expect others to do so?

Alumni remember their own student days in the afterglow of youthful sentiment and are inclined to idealize the university as it was. Their reaction is not unlike that of the man who received his education in the little red school, who now builds highways past its door for modern motor cars whizzing by at 30 times the speed of the horse and buggy which may have been his transportation, and who yet is annoyed at the suggestion that the old building must be replaced with a structure serving an enlarged community created by the motor car and the highway which he built.

While the alumnus is emotionally tied to the campus of other years, he also has a sense of the changing times in education. As a realist, he knows that the great forward march of America which has dramatically changed every aspect of the nation's life in his lifetime must affect education. He certainly does not want his alma mater to belong to the past.

We must try to make the alumnus understand the university as it is and as it must be, even while his greatest tie to us is his affection for the university as it was. He remembers the university which prepared his generation of students for the present, while the university must be continually concerned about preparing the present generation for the future.

Perhaps the beginning of alumni work is in having every undergraduate student understand the system of higher education in this country and its social significance.

In the history of our country the establishment of universal educational opportunity, the growth in support for the free public elementary and secondary schools, the establishment and development of our state universities and land-grant colleges, the founding of many non-public institutions in the public service, have all come only after terrific struggle for support and great battles in public debate.

But in each generation, the issues must be defined anew and the battles fought again.

It is a waste of time to cry about the inadequacies of our institutions or the unfairness of the way with which education is treated. We must set about to change the attitudes which will determine the future. In that task, the alumnus has a dominant part. He will rally to the call, if we are equal to the task of involving him meaningfully in the mission which has commanded our own lives.

NATIONAL VIEW OF HIGHER EDUCATION

A major weakness in the ways and means of public understanding of higher education is the lack of continuing machinery for effectively identifying for public analysis those issues affecting the welfare of all institutions. The efforts of most of us will be directed toward the interpretation of our own institutions and working with our own direct constituencies. But a university cannot live unto itself, and what happens to institutions across the land affects everyone in some measure. In turn, the welfare of each is a part of the whole. It is therefore to be regretted that higher education as a totality has inadequate interpretation.

It is true that common problems are discussed in educational meetings, and educators talk to one another about their concerns. Very often headlines develop from such discussions, but the resolutions of educational meetings are not sufficient to communicate to the American people what is happening, nor is the sensational headline of an individual critic.

To those who are vitally interested in any given subject, the evolution of national attention to that subject, even when it has to do with the welfare of the nation, seems tediously slow. The great population boom which at present is everywhere discussed and analyzed, and which we now know reaches into every part of American life, not just education, has been on the way for some time. The count of children has been available. School superintendents have been asking for more buildings and increased numbers of teachers, first for the elementary grades, then for the high schools. In higher education, the new numbers will arrive when present loads are difficult to carry. Deficits in facilities, faculties, and financing, occasioned first by the depression, then by the restrictions of wartime, then by postwar inflation, have not been met.

One of the most important unsolved problems in the relation of higher education to its public is the lack of machinery to give the American people a comprehensive, objective, multiple-dimensional view of their colleges and universities, and to do so repeatedly and continuously.

In many ways higher education today is in transition. In enrolment prospect, the population curve is at a low point before the predicted sharp ascent in the decade beginning in 1960. The vital relationship between the talents and abilities of college-trained people and the prosperity and security of a nation is only beginning to be broadly understood. The tremendous needs of educational institutions are collectively just now becoming clearly defined; and the waste of precious human talent not now brought to maximum usefulness has become a national concern.

It is a continuing task in interpretation to make clear that citizens must not take the narrow view that the welfare of universities and colleges is of concern to them only when their children are enrolled, or when the supply of trained personnel for their business is affected. The welfare, quality, integrity, and achievement of higher education are part of the heritage which we must hold for all of those who in the future will have need for its services.

Adults are not alone managers of the present, but trustees of tomorrow. Thousands are on the march to the campus of the future. We must prepare for them. Even for those who do not attend, the college opportunity must be available, so that the decision not to attend is a free choice, not one of economic selection or limited alternatives. Whether or not the child of today takes advantage of the opportunity of tomorrow, the existence of that opportunity is a major influence upon his own life, his attitudes, his hopes, his aspirations. It is a symbol of the public concern for the welfare of the individual. It is an index to the hope that he, too, may learn how to grow and to develop and prepare for any task for which he is capable.

The decision by the American people, made over the decades of early development, to establish private colleges and universities and to build the state university system and, more recently, municipal universities represented the acceptance of the ideal of making higher education available to all who could profit from it. That decision was one of heroic proportions and its full import has not yet been realized.

Certainly, considering the central place of higher education in the health, prosperity, and security of the nation, now is not the time to alter our goals simply because we have more people to serve. Higher education enrollments have doubled three times in the last fifty years, and we can make provision for their doubling again if there is popular conviction as to its importance and imagination enough in method and adaptation. Doubt as to an expanding role for education in the presence of an expanding America is a retreat from a position of confidence in the essence of democracy itself.

Let us assume that America will not accept a philosophy of dividing up what educational service it has instead of creating more. Educated men and women are America's chief resource, and the people will have the wisdom to develop it if they understand the issues. And I believe they are coming to understand the issues. The remarkable growth in the record of private giving to higher education, the formal declarations of organized business and organized labor, the increased attention to discussions of the problems of higher education are all hopeful signs that the climate of public opinion basic to adequate support will develop in time to enable the colleges and universities to meet their new obligations and new opportunities.

There is important work to do, and at the institutional level and at the national level lay participation in and understanding of that work is of primary importance. We must strive for a condition, says John Gardner of the Carnegie Corporation, which would have education as "our national preoccupation, our passion, our obsession."

The schools and colleges would then be the heart of a national endeavor, not, as Mr. Gardner says they now often find themselves, "swimming upstream against the interests of a public that thinks everything else more urgent."

We are held back not by lack of capacity or power. As a people, we can accomplish what we set out to do. Our choices, not our means, can be decisive.

A Concluding Note

In the wake of a national election, citizens generally feel the urgency of public decisions which are in the making. Throughout the campaign for the presidency, and at other levels of electoral decision, discussions reflected wide acceptance of the belief that the United States is entering a new era — an era of change, challenge and achievement beyond our present capacity to define.

Every component part of this national expectation is rooted in higher education. National defense and international security, economic growth, public health, cultural and social progress are all related to knowledge, intellectual discovery, leadership, professional service, and public intelligence. These in turn are directly dependent upon the health, strength, and productivity of the colleges and universities of the nation.

It is ironical that while the expectation for national growth and improvement is so high, so little public attention has been given to the educational means to that end. There are more recruits for the campus than ever before and there are more demands for graduates than ever before. The university laboratory has within it the hope of finding the cancer cure, or unlocking other secrets of science, or developing the methods of space technology. But a national program for strengthening higher education remains to be conceived, let alone written; and the state, local, and private constituencies of our several institutions are only beginning to understand what must be done. Recreation and luxuries command an increasing share of our resources as we try to decide how much to pay our teachers and how to put an educational roof over our heads.

But a "break through" in public understanding of educational issues may be noted. The unhappy alternatives to increased financial support are being recognized and the deliberations upon educational budgets for 1961 will be characterized by the feeling that we are working against time in facing up to what now must be done.

This mood is depicted in the recently released report of the President's Commission on National Goals:[1] "The development of the individual and the nation demand that education at every level and in every discipline be strengthened and its effectiveness enhanced."

On dollars for education, the Report states: "Annual public and private expenditure for education by 1970 must . . . double the 1960 figure."   Also, "a higher proportion of the gross national product must be devoted to educational purposes."

All of this is to the end that we shall "preserve and enlarge our own liberties, . . . meet a deadly menace, and . . . extend the area of freedom throughout the world."

To meet the challenge of the nineteen sixties, "every American is summoned to extraordinary personal responsibility, sustained effort, and sacrifice."

Published Sources

"Higher Education and the American Public" (reprinted from *Higher Education and the Society It Serves,* American Council on Education, Washington, D.C., 1957.)

"Implications of the Increase in Population of Major Consequence to Education" (*Program for A Look to the Future a Conference at W. K. Kellogg Foundation Battle Creek, Michigan, June 21, 22, 23, 1956,* pp. 46-54.)

"Institutional Cooperation and Coordination in Meeting New Responsibilities" (*North Central Association Quarterly,* Vol. XXXII, No. 4, April 1958, pp. 318-324.)

"New Priorities in Research" (*The Educational Record,* V. 41, No. 2, April 1960, pp. 148-153.). Also (*Regional Technical Meetings, 1959.* American Iron and Steel Institute, N.Y., 1959, pp. 163-171)

"Possibilities, Purposes and Priorities" (*American Alumni Council News,* September 1959, Vol. XXVII, No. 1, pp. 4-10.)

"Recurring Crises in Education" (address to Illinois Secondary School Principals Association October 4, 1955) *Education Synopsis* (New York University School of Education February-March 1956, pp. 4-6.)

"The Role of the Federal Government in Higher Education" (*Educational Record,* Vol. 40, No. 3, July 1959, pp. 197-203.)

"The State of the University." University of Illinois, Urbana, Illinois, December 1959.

"The State of the University — Some Points of Interest, 1958-59." University of Illinois, Urbana, Illinois, December 1958.

"An Urban University Organizes Off-Campus Service" (reprinted from *Adult Education for Everybody,* New York Adult Education Council, Inc., 1954.)

Notes

The Issue

1. President's Committee on Education Beyond the High School. *Second Report to the President, Summary Report,* July, 1957, Washington, D. C., pp. 16-17.

Introduction

1. *U. S. News and World Report,* May 18, 1959.
2. *Ibid.* (Murray Shields. "Business Adviser's Forecast . . . "), pp. 52-54.
3. *Ibid.,* pp. 58-59.
4. *Ibid.* ("Coming: Revolt by Local Taxpayers?"), pp. 41-43.
5. Lippmann, Walter. Address. Fifth Annual Dinner, National Citizens Committee for the Public Schools, March 19, 1954.
6. Calkins, Robert D. "An Economist Looks at Higher Education," American Association of Land-Grant Colleges and State Universities, *Proceedings, Seventy-Second Annual Convention,* Washington, D. C., November 10-13, 1958, p. 61.

Chapter II

1. President's Committee on Education Beyond the High School. *Second Report to the President, Summary Report,* July, 1957, Washington, D. C., p. 1.
2. de Kiewiet, Cornelis W. "Tomorrow Is Too Late," *The Educational Record,* V. 38, No. 3, July, 1957, p. 191.
3. Sarton, George. *Man's Right to Knowledge,* quoted in Annual Report of the Vice President for Research, 1956-1957, Cornell University, p. 48.
4. Clark, George L. *The Encyclopedia of Chemistry,* Reinhold Publishing Corporation, New York, 1957, p. xv.
5. Smith, Harold H. "Education and the Control of Evolution," *The Saturday Review,* January 8, 1955, p. 7 ff.
6. *Ibid.,* p. 7.
7. *Ibid.,* p. 39.
8. *The Ford Foundation Annual Report,* 1959, p. 10.

Chapter III

1. *Higher Education in a Decade of Decision,* Report of the Educational Policies Commission of the National Education Association, 1957, p. 122.

2. Gould, Samuel B. "The Challenge," *The Educational Record,* V. 36, No. 3, July, 1955, p. 205.

Chapter IV

1. Associated Press business news analyst, Sam Dawson.

2. Pusey, Nathan M. Address to the Economic Club of New York, quoted in *Champaign-Urbana Courier,* June 17, 1959.

3. *New York Times Magazine,* May 13, 1956, p. 15.

4. Berrill, N. J. "Crisis in Basic Research," *Think Magazine,* September, 1959, p. 34.

5. *Ibid.*

6. Auburn, Norman. "Life, Liberty, and Higher Learning," *American Alumni Council News,* September, 1958, p. 17.

7. Bunting, J. Whitney. "Industry and the Graduate School," *The Educational Record,* October, 1959, V. 40, No. 4, pp. 301-311.

8. American Council of Learned Societies. *Annual Report,* 1957-1958, New York, p. 5.

9. American Association of Land-Grant Colleges and State Universities. *Circular Letter,* No. 23, December 3, 1957.

10. Pusey, Nathan M. *op. cit.*

11. Killian, James. Remarks to the National Press Club, Washington, D. C., July 7, 1959. Quoted in American Association of Land-Grant Colleges and State Universities. *Circular Letter,* July 22, 1959, p. 12.

12. Bunting, J. Whitney. *op. cit.*

13. *The Efficiency of Freedom.* Report of the Committee on Government and Higher Education, Baltimore, Maryland. Johns Hopkins Press, 1959, p. 3.

14. Fenn, Wallace O. "Men in Orbit," address at the dedication of Burrill Hall, University of Illinois, September 8, 1959.

Chapter V

1. The President's Committee on Education Beyond the High School. *Second Report to the President.* July, 1957, Washington, D. C., p. 2.

2. *Ibid.,* p. 66.

3. *Ibid.,* p. 66.

4. Harper, William Rainey. *The Trend in Higher Education,* Chicago, University of Chicago Press, 1905, p. 128.

5. Heald, Henry T. Address at the Southern University Conference, Houston, Texas, April 4, 1957.

6. Schnieder, Herman. *The University and the Municipality,* Summary of the Proceedings of the First Session of the National Association of Municipal Universities, Bulletin, 1915, No. 38, U. S. Bureau of Education, Government Printing Office, Washington, D. C., 1915.

7. Gould, Samuel B. "The Dimension of a College," *School and Society,* March 2, 1957, p. 70.

Chapter VI

1. Heald, Henry T. "The Contribution of the State University to American Life," Proceedings, The Installation of David Dodds Henry, University of Illinois, Urbana, Illinois, 1957, pp. 65-66.

2. The President's Committee on Education Beyond the High School. *Second Report to the President.* July, 1957, Washington, D. C., p. 59.

3. Reitz, J. Wayne. Remarks at Council of Presidents, American Association of Land-Grant Colleges and State Universities, November, 1957, Denver, Colorado.

4. *Higher Education in a Decade of Decision,* Report of the Educational Policies Commission of the National Education Association, 1957, p. 118.

5. *Ibid.,* p. 122.

Chapter VII

1. Carnegie Foundation for the Advancement of Teaching. "Federal Programs in Higher Education," Summary of a Discussion by the Trustees of the Carnegie Foundation . . . reprinted from the 1956-57 Annual Report.

2. President's Committee on Education Beyond the High School. *Second Report to the President,* July, 1957, Washington, D. C., p. 98.

3. Harris, Seymour E. "College Salaries, Financing of Higher Education, and Management of Institutions of Higher Learning," *Bulletin* of the American Association of University Professors, Vol. 44, No. 2, Summer, 1958, pp. 589-595.

4. American Association of Land-Grant Colleges and State Universities. *Circular Letter,* No. 24, September 9, 1958, p. 4.

5. President's Committee on Education Beyond the High School. *op. cit.,* p. 83.

6. *Ibid.,* p. 83.

7. *Ibid.,* p. 81.

8. Long, John D., and J. B. Black, Jr. *Needed Expansion of Facili-*

ties for Higher Education, 1958-70: How Much Will It Cost? Washington, D. C., American Council on Education, 1958, p. 18.

9. Pusey, Nathan M. *The Need for Public Support,* paper delivered at the 41st Annual Meeting of the American Council on Education, October 10, 1958, Chicago, Illinois, pp. 5-6.

10. American Association of Land-Grant Colleges and State Universities. *Circular Letter, op. cit.,* p. 4.

11. President's Committee on Education Beyond the High School. *op. cit.,* p. 104.

12. "Washington Report on Medical Sciences," September 2, 1957, No. 533, and September 23, 1957, No. 536.

13. U. S. Department of Commerce *Annual Report,* Bureau of Public Roads, Fiscal Year 1957, Washington, D. C., Government Printing Office, 1958, p. 5.

14. Federal Aid Highway Act, 1958.

15. U. S. Department of Commerce. *op. cit.,* p. 5.

16. Statement to National Industrial Conference Board, October, 1958.

17. "How Modern Is American Industry?" Reprint, McGraw-Hill Publishing Co., September, 1958.

18. *New York Times,* November 4, 1958.

19. Carnegie Foundation. *op. cit.,* p. 6.

20. Folsom, Marion B. "Some Suggested Adjustments in the Use of Our Resources," reprinted from *Proceedings of the American Philosophical Society,* Vol. 102, No. 4, August, 1958, p. 327.

Concluding Note

1. *New York Times,* November 28, 1960, pp. 22-23.